"*The Emotional Side of Organisational Change* boldly delves in
looked, misunderstood, and messy aspects of chang
attempt to navigate a volatile and fast-moving future
provides practical, actionable, and solidly researched strategies to build the
necessary structure, vision, and support to win collective hearts and minds."
Dr Nicola Millard, *Principal Innovation Partner at BT Business CTO*

"Drawing on her extensive practical experience and academic expertise,
Jennifer delivers another must read on the topic of change. Approaching change
with structure and pragmatism, this book serves as a valuable springboard for
anyone managing, implementing, or navigating organisational change."
Mark Catchlove, *Director – Insight Group, MillerKnoll Global Research & Planning*

"As a professional that has dedicated her career to helping organizations
through change, Jennifer's insights are spot on. Change is about navigating
people, and their emotions, forward. So those factors cannot be ignored. As
the speed of change increases, so must the skill with which we enable it."
Kay Sargent, *Director of Thought Leadership, Interiors, HOK*

"This book doesn't just discuss change – it dives deep into the human experience behind it! Jennifer Bryan understands that transformation isn't just about
strategy or execution; it's about people. Too often, leaders discount the paramount importance of human-centered change and that's why this book is a
wake-up call. Jennifer's approach is a real, practical, and urgently needed. If
you want to drive change and create meaningful impact, every leader should
read this before leading their next transformation!"
Lou Robey, *Award Winning Lead Change Manager at BBC (APM Award 2013 & Change
Awards 2024), Keynote Speaker & Presenter of Podcasts "Voices on the Edge of Change"*

"Jennifer has written a book that directly addresses the most important challenge of our era – in an age of perpetual societal and technological change –
people still matter most! *The Emotional Side of Organisational Change* cuts through the
noise of change theory to deliver practical, honest, and achievable insights.
It should be on every leader's desk who wants to turn uncertainty into opportunity through empathy and clarity."
Guy Sorrill, *Managing Director of Sysdoc*

"Right now, we need leaders who can 'Stop, Breathe, Listen' like never before.
Jennifer's book pragmatically offers us an approach to change that fore-
grounds the emotions and enables us to make wiser choices."
Megan Reitz, *Associate Fellow at Saïd Business School, Oxford University and
Author of "Speak Out, Listen Up"*

"What an insightful, practical, and relevant guide to keeping your people and supporting them through change. Jen brings a wealth of experience across sectors, highlighting what truly works – as well as the often unseen blind spots – so we can all benefit from her hard-won insight. Definitely recommended if you're leading or navigating change."

Melanie Stancliffe, Employment Partner at Freeths

"Jennifer Bryan highlights the critical aspects of human behaviour that few dare to address – emotions matter when leading people. Refreshingly direct and practical, The Emotional Side of Organisational Change challenges the status quo and offers essential solutions for leading positive change. Bryan's message is vital; without it, we risk leading from a place of ignorance."

Paige Hodsman, Workplace (Behavioural) and Psychoacoustic Specialist at Ecophon Saint-Gobain

"If you want a book that truly gets what change feels like at work, this is it. What makes this book stand out is Jennifer Bryan puts people at the heart of organisational change – cutting through the jargon with honesty, clarity, and compassion. She shows that change isn't just about systems or strategy – it's about emotion, reaction, and real human impact. Practical, relatable, and refreshingly real, this book gives leaders the tools to lead change in a way that works for people, not just the boardroom."

Dana Denis-Smith OBE, CEO, Obelisk Support & Founder, First 100 Years

"Jennifer L. Bryan brilliantly unpacks the complex challenge of leading transformation for the futures without losing hope or momentum. She shows how lifelong learning turns leadership from a lonely journey into a powerful, shared adventure. Holistic change-making has never felt more exciting – it's time to step into the unknown together. I can't wait to begin!"

Urs Hauenstein, Ph.D., President of the World Leadership Foundation

"As Jennifer says, we're entering a period of unprecedented change – driven by generative AI, global disruption, and shifting societal norms. The challenge isn't just technological – it's deeply human. In this timely and practical guide, Jennifer Bryan cuts through the noise to focus on what really matters: people. 'Change is about people, not rocket science' – and this book gives leaders the tools and mindset to navigate that truth with clarity, empathy, and purpose. If you're leading change in a world that won't stop changing, read this."

Dave Coplin, CEO & Founder, The Envisioners Ltd.

"Jen clearly articulates real world examples of good and bad change through her own (extensive) experience. This is not just a book about change, it's a manual to help lead change managers through the process. Reflective questions at the close of each chapter engage the reader to apply their new found knowledge to their own experience. A great addition to the change toolkit!"

Sophy Jacob, Project Manager at BBC Birmingham

"Jen's book is a standout resource for anyone leading people through transformation. It's insightful, grounded in real-world experience, and full of practical tools that actually work. She brings clarity to the complexity of change, while never losing sight of the people at the heart of it. A valuable guide for today's leaders."

Steve Green, *Past President of Association of Change Management Professionals UK Chapter*

"Jennifer Bryan delivers a powerful blend of personal insight and professional expertise, providing practical, actionable strategies essential for navigating change in our rapidly evolving, post-AI and post-pandemic world. At the heart of her compelling message is a vital truth: without deeply understanding the emotional, and often irrational, ways people respond to change, true leadership and successful transformation remain elusive. Jennifer's courage in sharing her personal journey illuminates her motivation and her pioneering role in placing human experience firmly at the centre of organisational change. Her approachable coaching style, enriched by decades of frontline experience, is evident in the thoughtfully crafted reflective questions and key takeaways concluding each chapter. This book is the roadmap for any change professional committed to leading genuinely effective, human-centred transformation."

Nilema Bhaka-Jones, *Co-Founder and CEO of Courageous Leaders*

"Jennifer brings rare clarity to the part of change we too often overlook at cost: the emotional experience. Yet it's critical for successful change. She reframes what it means to lead transformation – balancing the emotional and the rational, with practical tools. For anyone leading through complexity, Jennifer offers a vital, human-centred approach that is both urgently needed and deeply wise."

Charlotte Talmage, *Founder and CEO of Uuna*

"Jennifer Bryan brings a powerful, humane approach to the reality of leading change today. In *The Emotional Side of Organisational Change*, she reminds us that successful transformation isn't just about systems, processes, and strategies – it's about connecting with hearts and minds. Her holistic approach is insightful and innovative. It provides a practical guide for any leader ready to embrace authenticity, emotional intelligence, and sustainable change. A must-read for those who believe the future of work must be human first."

Talita Ferreira, *Seasoned Executive Director, NED and International Trainer and Coach for Directors and Executive Leaders*

"All too often organisational change is seen as a simple process, just follow these steps and you will get to your North Star. Jennifer's book calls out this over simplification, highlighting the need to really consider the full emotional spectrum that change evokes. If you are looking for a heart-felt, practical guide to really support your people, then this book is a must buy!"

Bex Moorhouse, *Global Head of Strategy, Ops Excellence & Performance-Procurement & REWS at WPP*

"In a world obsessed with performance and productivity, Jennifer Bryan dares to ask the deeper question: how do people really feel about change? This book is a wake-up call for leaders who are brave enough to lead with empathy, honesty, heart and aren't afraid to navigate uncertainty. Jennifer brings a rare blend of lived experience, practical wisdom, and deep emotional intelligence to the conversation on change. The result? A guidebook that doesn't just help you survive transformation, it helps you thrive through it. If you want to build resilient teams and lead meaningful change, you need to read this book."

Mark Leruste, CEO & Founder of StoryCast and bestselling author of Glow in the Dark

"This book is a timely reminder that successful change demands more than comms plans and KPIs; it demands emotional fluency, empathy, and the courage to listen to what's not being said. For those of us working at the intersection of business, science, and the human condition, Jennifer's work is not only refreshing, it's essential. The future of leadership, as I often say, will belong to the emotionally literate. This book gives them a solid starting point."

Scott D McArthur, The Consulting Futurist, Trainer, Facilitator, "Find Your Fire" Coach & Lecturer

"You may be wondering what emotions and change have in common? Why do we need to read this book? Whether people encounter a positive or negative experience with change, it creates a memory that shapes how they will respond to future changes they will encounter. The Emotional Side of Organisational Change: How to Survive and Thrive is a guide for organizations, managers, and change professionals to enhance their skill set. It offers practical, realistic scenarios, solutions, and summaries to help the reader. Jennifer is a well-qualified and talented leader of change with global recognition. I highly recommend her text because it is more than theory – it is based on experience. Regardless of your tenure with change (beginner, moderate, or expert), she has written a fast read that provides the right level of depth as a refresher or to leverage on your change journey."

Douglas Flory, (CCMP), Board of Directors, The Association of Change Management Professionals Global ACMP (2020-2023)

"The Emotional Side of Organisational Change: How to Survive and Thrive is a must-read for future-fit leaders. Jennifer Bryan flips the script on change, shifting it from a task to complete to a human experience to lead. She challenges leaders to treat change as an investment, not a cost, and backs it up with sharp insight and real-world stories. A practical guide for anyone ready to build resilient, human-centred organisations – and prepare for multiple possible futures. In a world where change is business as usual this book is essential reading."

Siân Harrington, Award-winning HR and Leadership Journalist, Editorial Director at The People Space and Future of Work Commentator

"What can I say. Change always has an 'emotional side' which, sadly, is never really taken that seriously by those who prefer frameworks and data to guide them on their change journey (not that they don't help). Emotions in change are critical to address the issues that are felt by the people who are impacted. The understanding that 'people are what matter during change' is critical and is sadly often displaced by those who lead change from a technology perspective. How can you make sure the technology works if you don't get the emotional buy-in from the people who are going to use it? This book helps to get under the skin of 'emotions' and, in my humble opinion, is a very worthwhile read."

Ron Leeman, Founder/Owner of the Highway of Change

"Change in life is inevitable – thriving is optional! This is a compelling read and insight for every leader to have in their toolkit, at any stage in their change journey."

Alex Stanforth, Record-breaking adventurer, international keynote speaker and founder of Mind Over Mountains

"Jennifer Bryan masterfully highlights the often-ignored emotional side of change. Her work is essential reading for any leader who truly wants to build resilient, future-fit organizations. This book doesn't just teach change — it transforms the way you think about leading people through it."

Alan Furley, Co-Founder & CEO, ISL Talent

"Jennifer Bryan has written a timely and provocative understanding of the importance of change in all aspects of our lives: not just business but how our personal lives privately and professionally are affected. We derive communication from our attitudes and emotions. Change is brought about by the delivery of these tools around the urgency of change. Kudos to Jennifer for her dedication to bringing this critical topic to the forefront into today's chaotic turmoil globally."

Stanley Zareff, Communications Coach, Zareff Consulting LLC

"This is a book about change for people who have a day job (and a life) to be getting on with. Jennifer telescopes between the macro trends in the world and the ordinary day-to-day "so what" we all face – as we try to get things done in a way that makes sense to us. At the heart of her message is a mantra I've heard from her many times over the years: "It's the people, stupid!" And that means paying attention to what people, and ourselves, are actually thinking and feeling, not what others think we should. Which leads to her top three tips that a leader can do tasked with leading change: "Stop. Breathe. Listen."

John Higgins, Researcher, Author, Editor, Advisor

"Jennifer Bryan has written a powerful and necessary guide that speaks to the soul of change. *The Emotional Side of Organisational Change* reminds us that transformation isn't just about strategy – it's about stories, emotions, and the people behind them. This book is a must-read for leaders who want to create meaningful, human-centered change."

Preethi Nair, *Author, Story Coach & Founder of Kiss the Frog®*

"What Jennifer Bryan doesn't know about change isn't worth knowing. This book finally puts people, not process at the heart of transformation."

Alex Merry, *Public speaking coach and Founder of MicDrop*

"I had a pleasure working with Jennifer on a large workplace project, and this book definitely covers what you deal with the most in the daily practice of change management. Successful change is 60% about getting buy-in and managing everyone's emotions. And handling emotions doesn't mean abandoning rational communications – but you need to keep your hand on the pulse of the population."

Maciej Markowski, *CEO of SquarePlan*

"Jennifer Bryan is an experienced change manager with her practical approach to change captured in her previous book. This second book offers a refreshing focus on the emotional and human aspects of change, Jennifer provides practical tools, insightful case studies and recommendations to help leaders create better human-centric organisations. This book is a must-read for leaders and managers who recognise that their workforce are their biggest asset."

Dr. Nigel Oseland, *Chartered (Environmental) Psychologist, Workplace Consultant, Change Manager, Applied Researcher, Author and International Speaker*

THE EMOTIONAL SIDE OF ORGANISATIONAL CHANGE

Most people shy away from emotion, especially at work. Yet, when it comes to leading change, emotion is exactly what leaders can't afford to ignore. This book lifts the lid on the part of change leadership that's so often overlooked: how people **feel**. It explores why emotions drive behaviour, how they shape reactions to change, and what leaders can do to turn emotional resistance into resilience and momentum.

Change has become business as usual but that doesn't mean leaders know how to manage it well. Too often, feelings are dismissed, ignored, or avoided altogether, leaving people demotivated and disengaged. And change is no longer a one-off event; it's constant. Every leader, regardless of role or industry, needs to navigate shifting priorities, structures, and expectations. But while the pace of change has accelerated, our ability to deal with its emotional impact has not. This book offers a proven, people-first approach to leading change that works and puts understanding, empathy, and foresight at the heart of the process. Drawing on cutting-edge behavioural research and tested in organisations around the world, *The Emotional Side of Organisational Change: How to Survive and Thrive* is both practical and powerful. It combines foresight tools like horizon scanning and trend analysis with organisational development insights to help leaders design change that sticks for both the business and the people within it.

Whether you're a functional business leader, HR professional, or change-maker, this book shows you how to navigate constant change with confidence, lead people through uncertainty, and build an organisation that's truly future-ready.

Jennifer Bryan uses the end person in mind perspective along with her unique holistic approach to change to help leaders put people at the heart of decision, enabling them to save money, make money and increase staff satisfaction. She has over 25 years of experience working with a multitude of organisations such as Microsoft, Gartner, Barclays and more. Jennifer is an award-winning leader, TEDx and international speaker and highly renowned change expert in the industry.

THE EMOTIONAL SIDE OF ORGANISATIONAL CHANGE

How to Survive and Thrive

Jennifer Bryan

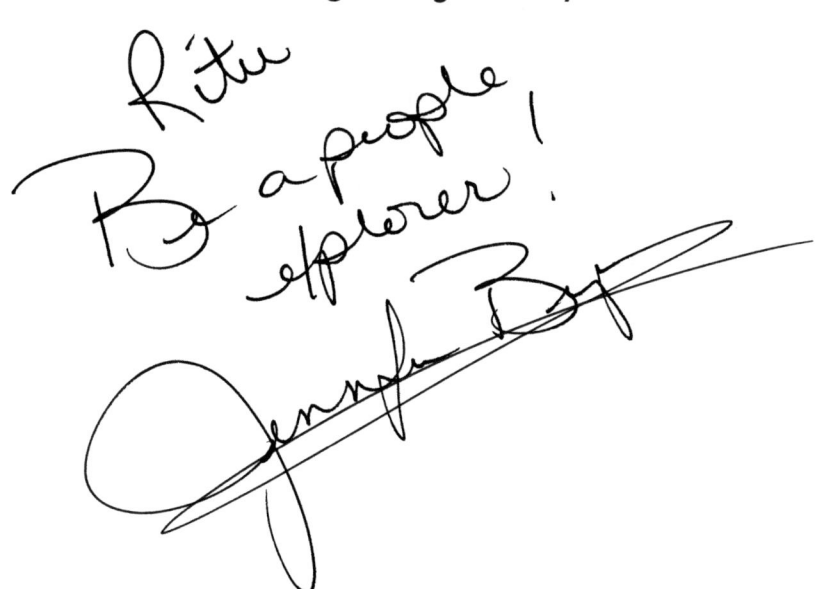

 Routledge
Taylor & Francis Group

LONDON AND NEW YORK

Designed cover image: Getty Images - koyu

First published 2026
by Routledge
4 Park Square, Milton Park, Abingdon, Oxon OX14 4RN

and by Routledge
605 Third Avenue, New York, NY 10158

Routledge is an imprint of the Taylor & Francis Group, an informa business

For Product Safety Concerns and Information please contact our EU representative GPSR@taylorandfrancis.com. Taylor & Francis Verlag GmbH, Kaufingerstraße 24, 80331 München, Germany.

British Library Cataloguing-in-Publication Data
A catalogue record for this book is available from the British Library

ISBN: 978-1-041-08090-9 (hbk)
ISBN: 978-1-041-06755-9 (pbk)
ISBN: 978-1-003-64369-2 (ebk)

DOI: 10.4324/9781003643692

Typeset in Joanna
by SPi Technologies India Pvt Ltd (Straive)

CONTENTS

FOREWORD

By John Higgins, April 29th, 2025

Change always exists in the eye and heart of the beholder, there is never a single view. It is understood and engaged with in ways that make sense to whoever is involved on their own terms, however much others try and impose their perspective and what they see as a desirable definition.

We all find our own language, our own framing, our own philosophy for going about our lives – some of us coming from a position of good faith, while others stay stuck in bad faith, in existentialist terms actively choosing our lives while others hide from the responsibility of choice. Change happens in the midst of our lives, not as some separate experience bolted on from outside. It happens while we are getting on with the everything else, often evoking or amplifying historic patterns invisible to others.

In this book Jennifer dares to be personal and straightforward. I was caught short as I read through it, wanting to argue about, insist upon, a more complex and nuanced approach. I wanted her to enter into the vortex of the debate about the labelling of change – and therefore missed her point, that we need to be less concerned about the theoretical framing of change and much more focused on how people actually feel and experience it on their own terms.

By being both heartfelt and grounded in people's day-to-day lives, she invites the reader to explore their individual pragmatics for making sense of change in the workplace and how this draws upon and ripples out into all aspects of their lives. What happens at work doesn't start and end there, you can't put change in a box and tell it to stay there. She avoids retreating into conceptual abstraction, staying true to a guiding principle that takes seriously the day-to-day of our lives, and the emotional experience of leading and being led in the world as it is for us – not as others think it should be.

Echoing her own background on the stage, her approach to change brings to my mind the widely used instruction from the world of Musical Theatre: "Once more. With feeling!" Ironically the overuse of the term passion in the corporate sector has stripped real feeling out of the change lexicon. To understand change is to understand human feeling.

With my perspective that all change is personal and that individual, first-person experience needs to be made much more figural than most of the change literature allows for, what I particularly enjoy is her willingness to anchor this feelingful orientation to change within her life and history – which like all lives has elements of the ordinary and the extraordinary. To understand our relationship to change, it is not enough to have grand theories about the motivation of others, we have to understand ourselves. In Jennifer's case, she does this not through a litany of grand achievements and set-piece setbacks (from which she triumphantly recovers), but by telling stories from everything she's experienced, as both younger and older Jennifer.

And she doesn't sanitise or distance herself from these experiences, as I often do, by holding herself at arm's length from their intensity through the distancing language of the psychoanalytic tradition. Of course, there is a time and a place for such approaches, but they are often overused, as part of the tradition that wants to invert the theatrical phrase above to read: "Once more. Without feeling."

For me Jennifer's work is an extension to Brene Brown's "Dare to Lead" philosophy. Jennifer invites us to dare in two ways – to dare both to feel and to be ordinary, where I am using ordinary not in a pejorative sense but as a reminder that we all know about the experience of change, but possibly not using the language of the professional change industry. As she has said many times: "Change isn't rocket science."

Above all, this means owning the partiality of our understanding of any situation and the emotional heft that change can evoke in us and others. This has very little to do with the grand plans of those who only see change from the top of the mountain. From that perspective, the lives of others are impersonal dots to be moved/manipulated this way and that, rather than flesh and blood human beings, living lives which experience change – to borrow from the title of the 2011 movie – as "Extremely Loud and Incredibly Close."

John Higgins is an independent academic and co-author of numerous articles for the Harvard Business Review and Sloan Management Review. His latest books are *Speak Out, Listen Up* with Professor Megan Reitz and *The Great Unheard at Work* with Dr Mark Cole.

INTRODUCTION

Many may ask why I am writing another book on leading change and the reason is simple. Emotions are a part of ALL change, whether that change is personal or professional, and yet they are rarely discussed. When change happens in the workplace, managers need to be able to address/manage and handle emotion rather than ignore or avoid it. This is complicated because people are typically afraid of having to face emotions, in life, as well as the workplace. As a result, managers most of the time pretend it does not exist or avoid emotions at all cost until it gets to the point they cannot ignore it any longer.

So how do we deal with emotion? It is personal and the Kubler-Ross change/grief curve is really the only model that has been used to talk about emotion in a change context and that was created in 1963. However, change is very different since that model was created – it is now constant and continuous. It is also happening at the fastest rate it has ever done so, and is projected to only get faster.

Throughout my time working, speaking, researching and coaching people in change, it has become blindly obvious that despite the numerous existing change books, models and theories out there, leaders still struggle to manage change and I think that is because we struggle to deal with emotion – particularly other people's emotions.

So the answer in how we address and manage emotion in change is to use the holistic approach with the end person in mind perspective and this is a game changer.

My typical approach and way I express myself in business is many times unemotional because that is how I was brought up. But I have learned that does not do myself, the situation or others any favours. In fact, it has been my experience that it does the opposite – it creates more problems and can make what starts out as small problems into bigger ones.

You know the phrase, "Don't make a mountain out of a mole hill"? The difference here is what may appear or seem like a mole hill to you, can easily be a mountain to someone else.

When I was growing up, my emotions were continuously invalidated, under-valued and dismissed – I mean constantly dismissed and this continued well into adulthood. The phrase that was regularly used was "Oh Jennifer" which was a tactic that immediately dismissed whatever it was I was saying at the time. In addition, because many of my thoughts and ideas were contrary to the sexist, conservative home, I was labelled by my grandmother as giving "sass," by my mother as "difficult" and my father "argumentative." When this happened, I would get angry because although my thoughts and feelings may be contrary to others, this did not mean they were worth any less. However, the problem with me getting angry was this did not help or make the situation any better. Instead, the situation would get worse for myself and for others because it would immediately put us at a discourse that was not addressed and so no compromise or acknowledgement was given.

As a result, I have had to learn how to express not only my emotions in a way that did not evoke anger in myself, but to also be aware of other people's emotions and how those are manifested. Many times people do not verbally articulate their emotions for a whole host of reasons. There are other ways though emotion is expressed in what is not said and how it is not said and what people don't do and how they don't do it. When we start to understand this, we can start to manage change more effectively because we will be actively using a people-centric and empathetic approach to change.

In 2023, there were 72% more corporate bankruptcies than there were in 2022 (Daniel 2024)! 642 corporations did not change and adapt, so now they NO LONGER exist. Dyson's electric cars project lost £500m and Nike's ERP upgrade cost them an extra $100m all due to project mistakes (Igbinoba 2023).

IT IS TIME – to start to realise that managing change the way we have done it before no longer works. A new mindset is required which creates new behaviours and builds new skills. Leaders need to plan change for the future with the end person in mind – an empathetic people focus, not a task focus, which has been the traditional way of approaching change. "We want to do x, so lets put the things in place to do x. Oh, by the way, we need to tell people what we are doing, so let's send out some communications…hmmm might need some training. Better get a change person in." The number of times I have heard that thought process is countless, and according to my colleagues, I am not alone.

"We are completely complacent with our thinking" (de Bono 2009, pg. 1). No amount of burying the heads in the sand will do anymore. $260 billion was lost in unsuccessful development projects in 2020 (Kingsmen Software Blog 2021)! That is a very high number and that is only one type of change. Can you imagine how much higher the number would be if we were to calculate all failed or unsuccessful change in all industries within any one given year? I cannot begin to fathom. And yet many leaders keep managing change as if it is all just hunky dory and believe that it is not them that need to change, but everyone else.

If it is one thing I have learned, it is that change is about people not rocket science. Now that is not to say that change is simple – it is just that we sometimes make it more complicated than it needs to be. It is also not to say that people are simple because $A + B \neq C$, when it comes to people, like it does with rocket science, and leading change is about leading people.

Now this may sound obvious, but typically leaders will focus 80% of their time on the tasks of change (project plans, budgets, communication plans, etc.) and only 20% of their time on people. When in reality the reverse is required: 80% of the time they need to focus on the people and 20% on the tasks (that is why all change leaders should and usually have a change team – to delegate). This is even more prevalent with the adoption of generative AI (but more on that in Chapter 2).

The reality is, change is part of our everyday business, but many of us do not have a clue how to manage it, so it is successful and generates a good investment rather than a loss. Change should help the bottom line and overall productivity of an organisation. It should and will not hinder it, **if** it is done right.

A clear case study illustrating the positive difference a people-focused approach takes with the bottom line can be seen with the financial

2013

Vision: "To create a family of devices and services for individuals and businesses that empower people around the globe at home, at work and on the go, for the activities they value most."

2016

Vision: "To empower every person and every organisation on the planet to achieve more."

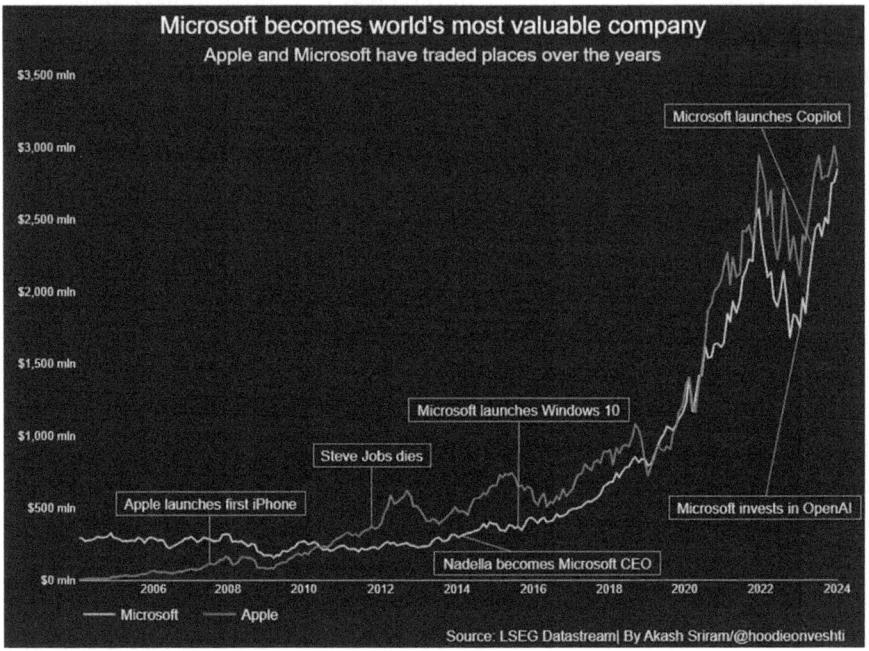

Figure 0.1 Organisational impact of having a people focus vision.
https://www.reuters.com/technology/microsoft-overtakes-apple-worlds-most-valuable-company-2024-01-11/

performance difference of Microsoft between 2013 and 2016–2024. You can see that back in 2013, Microsoft's mission was focused more on products and services. Additionally, their financial performance always trailed a great deal behind Apple, one of their greatest rivals (Visnji 2019). Then in 2016, a new mission was created that got rid of the products and services focus and completely and utterly focused solely on people (see figure 0.1). Suddenly the financial difference between the two companies was not nearly as great and there have been several times when Microsoft, as a result, have toppled Apple's financial performance (Richter 2024).

29–48% better organisational performance is what happens when leaders are "more human" (Gartner 2024). What does that mean? According to Gartner, it holds down to three things (2024):

1. Authenticity which is demonstrated through role modelling.
2. Empathy which is demonstrated through caring about others.
3. Adaptability which is demonstrated through giving flexibility and support to others.

We may know in our heads that we need to be authentic, empathetic and adaptable and hence this may not seem like completely new information, but the reality is we rarely put these things into practice. Instead, we typically focus too much on the task of things and less on the people, when we need to do the exact opposite. This can be seen clearly in the performance management processes that are used within organisations. How you reward, give feedback and measure success will determine whether you are able to focus on people or tasks.

For example, during a collaborative research project with Henley Business School of Management, one of the members stated that she was struggling to use a people focus approach because the change she was leading on would take 3-5 years to complete (this is not unusual, as I am sure you have experienced). As a result, many of the key milestones would not be achieved until year 2-3; however, she was performance-managed on an annual basis. Based on this and their system, she said she would be penalised because it would look like she had not "achieved" anything within the first year of the programme.

So our internal systems and processes play as much of a role in how we lead and manage because that drives the behaviours and mindsets within the culture of the organisation. When Satya Nadella took over the management of Microsoft, he changed the vision and culture of the organisation, which also included changing the systems in processes because he knew that this would drive different behaviours and create a different culture within the organisation.

Now this is not to say that having a complete people focus will make change easy or easier to manage because it won't. People are complicated and emotional, and this has a huge role to play, but leaders who are building and managing organisations that are going to survive into the future will need to be able to manage the human complications and emotions, as well as be comfortable with them.

So, to be clear, you are NOT a change leader for the future if you view change from a very narrow perspective. Instead your perspective needs to include a wide range of people (if it is an organisational transformation – then everyone in the organisation), along with internal and external influencing factors, which is explained more in Chapter 5.

For decades, it has been agreed that change is a constant and for a whole host of reasons, which we will discuss more later, it feels like it is getting faster and faster. So doesn't it stand to reason that before a change or crisis happens or needs to happen, an organisation should have the ability/resilience to transform?

In the McKinsey report, "The Resilience Imperative: Succeeding in Uncertain Times", resilience is defined as, "the ability to withstand unpredictable threat or change and then to emerge stronger" (Nauck et al. 2021). In other words, it is the ability to sustain and endure.

But how do we build resilience? How do we make sure we are ready, as an organisation, to deal with whatever comes down the road?

Previously, in business, we have talked about embedding, enabling, and/or adopting change to describe and illustrate a change that is long-lasting – sustained. However, that does not mean that the change itself does not change. In order for it to genuinely be sustainable, it has to have the ability to exist and metamorphosise to meet the changing needs of the business, based on the external and internal factors that influence an organisation and change.

Typically change programmes are conceived using hindsight and thrown into a changing world, yet many fail to use leading-edge data to inform live change programmes and as a result they fail to bring the people along with them, which is critical for any change success.

The purpose of the collaborative research project with Henley Business School of Management was to take a look at how change programmes can use "informed adaptability." In other words, to make good decisions in the here and now to inform live change by gaining insight about the changing world to inform and activate adaptability (Bryan et al. 2023).

In order to conduct this research, member organisations volunteered to participate. It was a priority to obtain different types of organisations in different industries and sectors to illustrate the breadth of the theory, so a total of four organisations took part: two public and two private sector organisations. There was a kick-off workshop to share all the models, tools, tactics and theories incorporated into the approach, along with agreed expectations and rules of engagement.

To begin with, adopting foresight means taking the view that the future is not predictable, nor is it predetermined – it is shaped by human action. Neither does it aim to unveil the future but it does help us build it (Szostak 2021).

The key challenges the members faced were:

- Changing priorities and personnel which affected people's capacity and focus on the future.
- Short-term organisational rhythms would hinder the adoption of foresight in change (this was described earlier with a performance management system).
- The span of control and influence was seen as problematic (stakeholder management was constrained to the project team).
- The focus on the "here and now" with products and services rather than how the people's needs might change in the future.
- There was the choosing of the "easy" tools and treating them as a task/to-do list, rather than as part of a toolkit. Thus limiting a change in behaviour and impact in leading change overall.

With that said though, what they did find useful and what was clear was that the approach did:

- Help to aid in conversations; it got them started and created a trusting environment.
- Highlighted many "unspokens" – it clarified where there were some blockages and would help open their eyes to some previously held blind spots.
- Help create a fuller picture of what is actually going on in the organisation. They are now noticing different things that they had not picked up before.
- It also really helped in decision-making by setting priorities and using the tools as metrics in the change programme.

The reality is that most people are not aware of how they are engaging with the future. They don't realise that by not engaging with it they are allowing it to happen "to them" not "with them." And yet that is exactly how we can change what is to happen – with us. So, we need to engage with the future more deliberately, using a range of methods to get to know and shape the future. Also what is really clear is this is not easy, as we said earlier. It takes practice, practice, practice.

My big motivator is to help – that is why I get up in the morning. So my aim with this book is to help you lead your people in change so you, your team, your colleagues and your organisations are ready and able to thrive and deal with whatever comes down the road.

In this book you will receive clear practical tools, advice, guidance and examples on just how you can lead change in an unpredictable world whilst surviving the emotional side of change that is unavoidable. It focuses entirely on the people aspects and the difference good, intentional leadership can make to people going through business change. We will discuss the big elephant in the room, biggest disruptors of our time, how we can create psychological safety for our teams, build sustainable change, build a community of change and create plans that are going to take into account a holistic approach that enables us to be resilient as a whole: people and organisation.

Because IT IS TIME to start to get change right. To put people at the heart of your decision-making. The world may feel like it is going extraordinarily fast and is very uncertain, but I can guarantee you one thing: in this moment, the world is moving the slowest and is the most certain than it will ever be, so let's use this time to reflect, learn and build, so we can lead our people into the future.

As Edward de Bono said, "You can analyse the past, but you need to design the future" (2009). So let's build a future that is people centric, enables us to navigate the emotions in change and is sustainable, so we can hold our heads up high and be proud of the work we do.

1

ELEPHANT IN THE ROOM

Be bold but respectful.

Pat Mitchell

Silence. Not saying or doing anything is still saying and doing something. When you ask someone a question, and they don't answer you – not because they did not hear you, or did not see/read your question; the answer they are giving you speaks volumes, particularly when leading change.

The challenge to us is, can we hear the response we are receiving in the silence?

Whenever I ask a question either verbally or face to face and I don't get an answer, I immediately start to think why – what is going on here that I might be missing. In the past, many times, I would ask the "why" question straight away. The problem with that is asking someone "why" can be seen as quite confrontational, so I have learned to try and take that thought away with me and reflect on it first, or try and ask a slightly different question. Typically, I now only ask the "why" question if what I want to do in that moment is to be confrontational.

DOI: 10.4324/9781003643692-1

There is a popular narrative that Kotter stated back in 1996 that 70% of changes do not succeed (Kotter 1996). Now this is not supported by empirical evidence, and I think that is predominantly due to the fact that clear success measures are not outlined with change, thus rendering the question "what is success"? However, we do know that the rate of change continues to increase, and the reality is that this rate is not going to slow down; in fact, it is the slowest it will ever be now. We also know the impact that the way change is currently happening has on people is not good. There is a high degree of burnout, change fatigue, employee dissatisfaction and low levels of trust with leadership.

So, what do we need to do differently? Firstly, we need to start recognising change as "business as usual" and hence hardwire it into our organisational systems and in our mindsets. This means building adaptability, flexibility and to use the concept of April Rinne, "element of flux" (2021), in our organisations. This includes not just our systems and processes but most importantly our people and us.

Typically, it is very rare for a leader to think about how they are going to lead their people in the change and the impact it will have on them beyond the "things," at this stage. However, it is at this precise moment when we do need to think about the type of journey the people we have to lead through this change and the impact this will have on their professional and personal lives. What they might be feeling/thinking – not just about the change itself, although that is a good start, but also what do they think/feel about the company, the leaders/managers? What impact will this have on their home and family life? This is important to understand because none of us are impervious to isolating our feelings from work and home – there is a seeping of emotions that happens because we are all human and that has an impact. Simone Fenton-Jarvis calls this the "voice of the people" (2022).

As leaders, we need to be aware of these areas, not just because it is our duty to care on the mental health of our staff, but because this impacts how our business will survive and potentially thrive through this transition.

Think about it, how can we possibly build and implement a change plan that will involve people buying in to do things differently if we don't actually take their thoughts, feelings and situations into account. That is like saying to an A-level student they have to attend a certain university and study a certain course, even if that is not remotely what they want/like or capable of doing. It makes no sense and ultimately drives demotivation, increased stress and eventually depression. In a business sense, this is what drives people away from the organisation, which has a big impact on the organisational performance and costs. There are numerous articles highlighting the difference that high- vs low-performing staff have on an organisation's bottom line and ultimate success within the market. So why, in the name of change, would you potentially jeopardise an organisation's performance by not taking into account how your people are thinking and feeling about life, much less the change?

A financial services institution was going through a major workplace change where they were moving from three different buildings into a completely new campus. The workforce, in general, were quite excited about the move that would happen in a couple of years, and they wanted to be involved in shaping and creating the new space and how it would operate. They had several employee engagement groups across several disciplines, such as DEI, sustainability, technology, public enterprise, etc. It was important to give each of these employee engagement groups a voice and map out in the programme plan exactly what they would be doing and how, so that the support and resources needed were in place, as and when, this was required. As a result, their engagement activities were included in the overall programme plan, which, to be fair, made the plan quite big and felt a little intimidating for the Programme Director, but when the responsibilities were clearly highlighted, it became clear that the activities that involved the Programme Director were within expectations. The perceived "additional" activities were actually owned by and involved just the engagement groups. The purpose of pulling them all together into one plan meant that everyone knew who was doing what and when, so there were no surprises. Thus, creating a true collaboration for the change and giving the people a voice with accountability, making them the ultimate owners of the change.

Before we get into the details of what activities are involved in leading a people-centric change, we need to define what is meant by the term. The term "people-centric" is commonly defined in the care industry as

> Person Centred Care (PCC) as an approach to patients that embodies an individual's right to self-determination and highlights their role as an equal partner in the care exchange. Care and support that is guided by and organized effectively around the needs and preferences of individuals.
>
> (Lloyd et al. 2017)

In the academic world, it is defined more as "intentional behavioural change to improve academic performance is a process that involves progression through the use of a set of overt and covert processes. These involve a change in attitudes, beliefs, behaviours and mindsets" (Cunha et al. 2020). Is this all starting to sound familiar?

To apply this in a change setting, the best theory is the transtheoretical therapy (TTP) as defined by Prochaska and DiClemente (1982). They defined people-centric change as having five basic stages: "consciousness raising (feedback and education), conditional stimuli (counterconditioning, stimulus control), catharsis (corrective emotional experiences, dramatic relief), choosing (self-liberation, social liberation), and contingency control (re-evaluation, contingency management)." They go further to say that the first three stages (consciousness raising, catharsis and choosing) are verbal processes, whereas the last two (conditional stimuli and contingency control) are behavioural.

Now this all sounds fairly reasonable if not very academic verbiage, but in the real world, what this means, is what we have suspected all along – we need to involve people from the beginning so they can go through the mental processes that are required with change, and this entails verbal, cognitive and behavioural elements.

When we are looking to build resilient organisations, we need to look beyond the standard focus areas with projects: having the mindset of "if they build it, the people will come" is not enough. It might have been the case back in the industrial age, when being told what to do was not only imperative to completing a task, but it was expected as a style of management in work. However, we are no longer in the industrial age, but in the digital and information age, and the expectations in the workplace are very different. People's expectations have also changed, particularly post pandemic – people are reviewing how they work and want more balance and are demanding more. And that's just the tip of the iceberg.

At the same time, being resilient is not about knowing exactly when or where the next disruption will come from, so it can fully be planned. It is about being able to understand all the different factors that could have an impact, so adjustments/amendments or completely new plans can be put in place quickly, to help people and organisations flex and adapt to changing environments. To sum it up, resilience is "not waiting for the storms to pass, but learning how to dance in the rain" (Green 1992).

A McKinsey report states (2022) that in 1958 the average life span of an organisation was 60 years; now that is 12 years, and in 2027, 75% of organisations listed will no longer exist – they will either be bought out, merged or gone bankrupt. This is a startling statistic that clearly illustrates that organisations need to change and adapt or die. Leading change can be tricky and feel bewildering, particularly when faced with the degree of uncertainty that is indicative of the current world. On top of that, leading people to ensure they are confident and supported to take business to the next level can also be and feel daunting. Many leaders believe people do not like change. If you think about it, this is not possible, as people deal with change all the time – a child is sick, so they have to quickly change what and where they work for the day, there is an accident on the road, so they have to change the route they were going to take to get to where they wanted to go, etc. But it is possible to say that people do not like **being** changed.

I was working with an agency within a Central Government Department that was about to move from a very dirty, old, dark and grungy building into a new bright, shiny, lots of light and amenities building. As we all started to pack up our work materials into boxes, we started to question how we needed to label them, to ensure the boxes got into the right area and place in the new building, as it was also really very big. It was at this time, 2 weeks prior to the actual move, that we found out we would not have allocated desks, like we did in the old building. Instead, there would be shared team spaces, and there would not be enough desks for every person. At the time, 85% of us had desktop computers for security reasons. So, it seemed impossible this new approach would work in the minds of everyone, including myself. As a result, many became quite upset, angry, anxious and overall negative about the move, after a time of great excitement. These thoughts, feelings and perspectives were so strong that multiple people, my colleagues, were complaining for 3 years after the move, even though the building was a 100% improvement and the shared space did not actually create any issues (Bryan 2021). That is the power of people not being taken on the journey of change and instead having change done unto them. Regardless of the positivity of the change, people will continue to perceive it negatively due to how it is delivered.

So, what does it mean to be a leader, particularly a leader in change? There are lots of different pieces of literature out there that define what constitutes a leader and what does not, but they can be quite different in their definitions. Furthermore, in some organisations, it is stated that all employees are leaders; whereas in others, the role of a leader is reserved for someone in a hierarchical senior position.

So, what separates one person from being a leader vs another person? Most of us would agree that even though someone has a senior position in a company, it does not mean that they are necessarily a leader – or if that they are a leader, but not one we would aspire to or advocate. In which case, what does that mean?

Many people state that you can't be a leader if you don't have followers (Google/YouTube sole dancing man video). Whilst others state it is not about the number of followers but what you do and how you do it. So, what is it?

Being a leader is about being a role model for whatever it is the organisation or you are trying to achieve. I was asked to take over the management of a change programme within a financial institution due to the current change person having some personal challenges. Upon doing so, I was involved in delivering a number of different communication leadership briefings, and I was, at first, surprised to discover a reasonably high level of resistance to the behaviours required of the change from the senior leadership teams. This particular change was not only temporary, but well accepted as imperative to enable the bigger change that would happen further down the road. It wasn't until I was involved in building the Board briefing that it became obvious that the CEO was bought into the necessity of the change but only for others and not for himself. Instead, he was adamant about continuing to work in the way in which he had always done, which was in direct contravention of the behavioural change needed. Due to this lack of role modelling, the other senior leaders in the organisation felt they too could not adopt the necessary behaviours, which also then dominoed into line managers and staff feeling resentful of the change.

As a leader, there is a responsibility to role model desired behaviours and that is in a professional environment as well as a personal one. For example, when I was studying for my Master's degree, there were many times I had to sit behind a closed door to write a dissertation, which my toddler daughter did not understand or like. But I felt it was important not only for my education and career, but also for her own development. She needed to understand although she was extremely important, I could not always be available at her whim; she would have to instead be with the other parent on duty. I also wanted her to have the memory of her mother obtaining a degree, which is why it was extremely important she attended the graduation ceremony, as I wanted her to have the ambition for university and getting a degree. To this day, even though she was only 3.5 years old, she still vaguely remembers going to a place and "mommy walking on stage wearing a funny hat and robe over her dress."

A leader needs to stand slightly above the crowd and show a path or direction. That does not mean that you are always challenging the status quo because you could be showing the path of what good looks like in the status quo. It also does not mean that you may not stumble along the way because all paths have a few stones, sticks, twists and turns. They are never entirely smooth.

It is about taking ownership and responsibility for what you do and how you do it. It is accepting the fallacies and mistakes along the way and turning them into lessons for oneself and for others. Also, if you have followers, it is about protecting them – making sure they are ok and giving them the support along the path that they need.

As leaders, there is a responsibility and skill set we need to lead people in change from a basic level: we need to be perceived as leading, have compassion and integrity and be honest. To do these things, we need to understand where people are coming from – as stated earlier, what they are thinking and feeling about life, much less the potential change we are about to embark on. This affects the approach, tone and style of the change plans from start to finish. If we don't take these things into account, then we risk the change going horribly wrong, which we can no longer afford as an organisation. There is room for experimenting, so long as we articulate what we are doing and why. However there is no room for ignoring our greatest asset – our people – and bull dozing our way through a change. With that comes huge consequences that leaders and organisations can rarely afford.

I was working with a financial services organisation, and they had implemented a new process of conducting transactions, which on the surface would streamline tasks and be more efficient. However, the reality was very different. This "new process" was developed and implemented only in one area of the whole system, rather than taking into consideration all the different teams involved and how they did things. As a result, confusion, duplication and inefficiencies in abundance were generated. So, we brought everyone into the room to first give them a chance to "air their grievances/challenges" and then map out what and how the different tasks and activities are involved in conducting these transactions. Once this was all completed, we were able to discuss all the different elements together and come up with a solution that would not only benefit all the teams involved, but actually deliver more efficiencies than were originally targeted.

Just deciding to make a change and wing it does not many times produce the desired outcomes. We need to look at things differently, using a different mindset that includes a whole picture approach. To create greater efficiencies that are actualised, we need to take a people-centric approach.

Key points

- Cannot afford to continue to approach change in the same way as before – it requires a different mindset with a focus on people.
- People-centric focus on change is not as simple as just saying that is what we are going to do. There needs to be internal systems and processes to support it.
- Leading people needs to be intentional – we can no longer afford to "just wing it."

Reflective questions

1. How has change been approached in your organisation to date?
2. How have you approached change previously?
3. How can you build flexibility into your organisational systems and processes to be able to adapt to change on a constant basis?

2

THREE BIGGEST DISRUPTORS OF OUR TIME

Our challenge...is to take those unavoidable features of the future as given, and still build a world where all of us can flourish.

Daniel Susskind

We are at a cultural crossroads that we have not experienced for a century. Back in 1926, Henry Ford created the 5-day work week on the back of the production line. At that time, he had a choice as a leader: to either maintain the status quo of his employees working 6-7 days a week, which was typical of that time, and end up with a surplus of vehicles that he was not certain he would be able to sell; or to reduce the work week whilst maintaining the same salary for staff, so the company only produces the number of vehicles he is confident he can sell. He decided on the latter, and during the Great Depression, many other companies followed suit in order to survive the times. Now, a hundred years later, we all still work 5 days a week, regardless of the industry – it won't necessarily be the same 5 days, but it will be 5 days.

DOI: 10.4324/9781003643692-2

With the advancement of technology happening at a speed of knots and the societal shifts and realignments, catapulted by the pandemic, leaders have a decision: do we continue doing what we have always done or do we do something different? For example, do we embrace a 3- or 4-day work week, universal wage, hybrid working or a combination of all three? This is just the beginning.

So, in all honesty, how can we plan for the future, when we don't know what the future will entail, much less determine or make sure we are "fighting fit" or rather resilient? None of us have a crystal ball, so we don't know when, where or how the next disruption will come. But one thing we do know is there will be another disruption of some sort, so how can we plan for this and build our business at the same time, so we are part of the surviving 25%, as outlined in the McKinsey report earlier?

During the pandemic, so many leaders and organisations were concerned about "keeping the wheels on the bus" that they only implemented the changes that enabled basic operation to continue the status quo. Once the pandemic started to come to a close, there was an impetus to "get going again." This included starting all the changes/plans that were scheduled to happen prior to the pandemic along with the ones that were identified during and after. As a result, the motivation and mantra became "just do something/just get it done." The problem being that during this frenzy of "doing things," change is being done for the sake of it or just that – getting it done. There has not been any thought as to why the change is needed, why it is needed now, much less why should anyone care about the change. This then has greater ramifications on people and organisations because it is increasing change fatigue, burnout and destroying any potential goodwill there may have once been for the change because the people have not been heard/included/brought along the journey, all for the sake of "getting it done."

How can we shift the mindset from deciding to take the time to plan the change so we get it right, rather than just get it done?

The three most important things a leader can do are to **stop, breathe and listen**. Why? Because when you do these three things, you give yourself the ability to take a moment, which enables you to look around you and see what is going on. It allows you to take notice of things and people. And depending on how long you take that moment, it also gives you time to reflect which can give you insight into questions you already have and, in that moment, you are then able to discover the answers. So, before you do anything, just stop, breathe and listen – take that moment!

When I was pregnant with my daughter, I was made redundant within 1 week of telling my manager, and I was the only person in the whole company, at that time, who was being made redundant. Now at first, I went into panic mode and started to ask questions to uncover the potential reason for this sudden change, which was quoted as being financial. So, I went into a whirlwind of budgeting to show how I could still deliver within the "new" budget constraints that were outlined. When those solutions were turned down, that is when I finally stopped, took a moment, breathed and listened. I listened to what was not being said and how it was not being said. It was only then I realised that no amount of re-planning, budgeting, etc would solve the problem because the problem was me being pregnant, and so a new plan of action would be needed and prepared.

When it comes to business decision-making, many times leaders and people are battling between the differences of change vs stability. However, they are the same side of a slightly different coin and the impact of either one can evoke similar emotions, as a result. For example, when it comes to change, some people feel excited, anticipatory, happy whilst others feel anxious, stressed, nervous or scared. In regard to stability though, some people feel excited, anticipatory and happy, whilst others feel anxious, stressed, nervous and scared about it for a whole host of reasons. In other words, some people will have the same feelings about stability as others will have about change; and our feelings in general are also quite dependent, in both of these scenarios, on the details and specifics of our individual situation – the influencing impacts the specific scenario either change or stability will have on our lives.

So, change and stability may appear to be quite opposite concepts, and by definition are in many ways, but the emotion each one evokes is the same and that includes in business. Some people like change because it is new, different, something to explore or discover. Whilst others like stability because it is automatic, they are used to it, meets the status quo. On the other hand, some people don't like change because it is unknown, requires doing something differently, it feels weird. Then there are others who equally do not like stability because they feel it is boring, requires doing the same thing over and over, it feels traditional.

So as leaders in business, when we are talking about change or stability, we may be thinking that everyone will be feeling the same thing about either concept, as we feel ourselves. The reality is we need to be aware, whichever side of the coin you are talking about, people are going to feel differently about change and stability – not everyone will have all positive or all negative emotions with either concept, and I think we sometimes forget that.

We get caught up in the glitz and glamour of change and/or of stability and forget that there are real emotions that people will feel that will then determine their behaviours and thoughts with both scenarios and that will have an impact on performance.

There can be just as much resistance with stability as there can be with change. So as leaders, it is not necessarily about whether we choose change or stability as the direction of travel. It is about understanding the emotions people will have with both and plan and manage how we are going to help them in either scenario.

Technology

This is perhaps the biggest disruptor of our time because it is happening at such a speed of knots we sometimes struggle to keep up. AI is no longer far away in the future – it is here, now and is already starting to have a great impact on a variety of professions and hence professional lives. It is true that a great deal of jobs will no longer exist, but it is also true that a great many jobs will be created as a result of AI. 60% of the current jobs in the NHS did not exist when it started in the 1950s. However, the big challenge is that we don't have the luxury of a generation to get use to the transformation. Instead of 70 years of evolutionary change, we will have 7 years and that is a lot for anyone to deal with, much less lead and manage.

As a result, it is critically important that as leaders we focus our attention on our people. Their mental and physical health and well-being will make all the difference to our productivity rates during this catapult of change. Dex Hunter-Torricke said, "all technology change is people change" (2024). His statement makes complete sense, if you think about it, because technology is just stuff at the end of the day – it is only useful and can only make a difference if people use it and use it well.

The big question is, how do we take a people-focused approach to technology and generative AI? Firstly, it is to recognise that a phased approach is needed. It cannot be done as a big bang, and it cannot be done in isolation. It needs to be controlled, decisive and deliberate.

It also needs to be driven from the top if it is going to affect the whole organisation. Oh and by the way, any generative AI tool that is being implemented will affect the whole organisation. This is for the simple reason that the organisational technology change needs to be seen and believed as an organisational priority and the only way this will happen is if it is prioritised from the top. Behaviours will need to be role-modelled, resources will need to be allocated and given the time, space and budget necessary across the whole organisation. This is outside of the project or programme team. Ever try to implement a change, technology or otherwise, that affected the whole organisation and did not need to involve HR, or Communications, or Marketing, or business unit leaders, etc. No, of course not – you have to involve them all and the only way for you to be prioritised by those areas is for the change to be understood as an organisation's priority and the only way that happens is that it is communicated and agreed from the top.

Some argue that a bottom-up approach works best within their organisation when they are doing something innovative, which is fine. But as soon as that innovation needs to be integrated across the whole business, then a different approach is needed. None more so than with generative AI. Several organisations seem to be "trying out" AI in an effort to "see how it goes." The problem with this is there are major implications for the whole business with generative AI. For example, in November of 2023, *Sports Illustrated* made headlines for publishing articles written by fake AI-generated authors (Callahan 2023). There have also been multiple fake citations discussed in several business networks by ChatGPT. Furthermore, there have been major ramifications for people when MSN used a poll asking why people thought a woman was murdered and using headlines, such as "Useless at 42," when describing the late Brandon Hunter (Callahan 2023). This is only a very small sample of the destruction generative AI can have if a people's focus approach is not used.

There is an over-riding process for delivering people-centric technology change that encompasses two over-arching phases: readiness and enablement.

1. Readiness phase involves uncovering the change mindset and under-standing the digital capability. This requires full on assessments in all areas of the business from leadership to understand the level of capabil-ity, understanding and readiness to adopt and lead the change; under-standing of the level of readiness from the organisation in regards to culture and behaviour; understanding of the ability for the support functions of the business to support the change; understanding of the value, opportunities and challenges the technology will have on busi-ness units; to understanding the current state of the organisation's tech-nology infrastructure and ability to support the organisation in the change.

2. Enablement phase involves defining the pathways to success, delivering the change and having the adoption and sustainability tools in place. This requires leadership role modelling, putting all the required plans in place and developing the technology or AI council and in the change network in place; delivering the activities and engagements and ensure that 360 degree feedback is enabled to ensure people are fully involved and taken on the journey. Furthermore, continuous reviews will need to be implemented, which will include processes and systems to ensure full adoption, sustainability and flexibility to ensure resilience going forward.

Using the phased process will enable a people-focused approach to the change, which is highly critical and valuable to the organisation. Without the people approach to generative AI and technology, the company risks high staff turnover, loss of talent, a dip in organisational performance, to name a few, and that is before there is the discussion on the potential legal implications.

UN sustainability goals

The idea of an organisation stating a priority around sustainability has been around for a couple of decades, but the outlining of the 17 specific areas by the UN has called out elements that organisations, I would argue, previously ignored – not necessarily because they did not care, but more because they envisaged bigger priorities at the time. But now that is no longer possible.

As a result, organisations are having to review how they operate and function beyond the element of having recycling bins. They have to review their supply chains, their energy usage and where that comes from and how, working practices to ensure there is no poverty and there is gender equality, etc. But to make this all happen, there needs to be more than just new policies generated. It will require the consensus and cooperation of the people across the whole organisation at all levels to ACT and that is a different kettle of fish. It requires pro-activity, planning, and in many cases, re-creating strategies and processes.

Slave labour is one of the biggest challenges and one that many people do not realise is prevalent in nearly every product we purchase. Every piece of technology we use typically has a good deal of slave labour worked into the cost of the product because the mining of the minerals needed to create the chips. It is also the 3rd biggest crime, at the moment, and is expected to become the biggest in 10 years, according to Madeline Fitton, Modern Slavery Founder and Chair of the Business Services Association.

As leaders of organisations, it is our duty to ask challenging questions and help companies we rely upon to make the right investments in their resources in an effort of reaching the targets of the UN sustainability goals.

Societal re-alignment and adjustments

Now one could argue that there are continuous societal adjustments happening and they would not be wrong. The difference this time is that there is a great majority of people who are questioning exactly what they want in their lives and how, which includes their professional lives and hence work. The pandemic was a real catalyst for this, and despite there being a drive for some to try to put the genie back in the bottle, I am afraid this is just not going to happen and we need to ask ourselves the question of what we want to be as an organisation and how do we want to be thought of by our staff, colleagues, leaders, peers, clients, customers, etc. (more of this later on in the book). In HR and sometimes leadership development, we talk about the psychological contract between an employee and an organisation, and this is not the first time there has been a shift in this area. Before, in the 1980s, there was an understanding that when you took a job with a company, that was typically for life – i.e. the rest of your career.

Now you would most likely not do the same job for 40 years, but you would be with the same company. The economic downturn of that time changed all that and many people found themselves without a job or a profession. Although companies still award individuals for long service, it is now seen as a rarity rather than a norm. One could argue that there was a general shift for companies to focus more on the shareholders rather than the employees, and thus, the employees started to prioritise their own personal and professional goals over loyalty to a specific company. However, even during that timeframe, there was an accepted norm, regardless of whatever company you worked for, that you would work for 5 days a week and for knowledge workers, typically from 9 to 5.

That is no longer the case; people's expectations have changed, and to be fair, technology has enabled many of these expectations, just as it has enabled the expectations of organisations to change.

"92% of mainstream companies report that they continue to struggle with cultural challenges relating to organisational alignment, business processes, change management, communication, people skill sets, and resistance or lack of understanding to enable change" (Garton, Mankins and Schwartz 2021). Therefore, we will need to be creative, think more about horizontal development and take a bigger picture perspective that goes beyond just the numbers game in an organisation.

Many have heard of the analogy that change is a story or a journey. The two questions that you need to then ask are:

1. What story do you want to share? (vision)
2. How do you want to travel? (plans)

How to answer these questions is laid out in Chapters 4–6. However, it is important to talk about the story itself to help re-assure you that whatever your story is, you do not need to be afraid of the uncertainty that will be involved.

For example, when it comes to reading books/films/TV, some of us will like mysteries, others thrillers or crime or romance, etc. However, what is one of the things we like the most about these stories? When we think we know what is going to happen to the main character and then there is suddenly a plot twist. Bang, just watch the internet blow up when one of the big shows has a plot twist. We love it – the unexpected, the uncertainty/

unpredictability of it all. When the opposite happens and we know exactly what is going to happen, we many times get bored and switch off.

So why is it we get so scared, as leaders, when it happens in business? Why does the level of uncertainty, many times, paralyse us into action and decision-making?

Typically, because we think of the negativity that is also linked to uncertainty – the inability to be able to control what exactly is going to happen and how. We feel that in business, we need to be in control, but the reality is we are never actually fully in control – we are just fooling ourselves, really.

So let's put a different spin on this and instead think "what could happen from a positive perspective." Uncertainty allows us to be creative, innovative; to test and explore. We did not know what the moon was like until we explored and tested our ability to go find out. Let's start asking the question, "how else can this be done?"

Dex Hunter-Torricke, who is Head of Communications and Marketing at Google DeepMind, said at the CIPD Festival of Work in 2024:

- The future of work is not the narrow application of apps.
- We need to nurture the collaboration between people and AI.
- We need to continuously evolve.
- Accept that change will outstrip imaginations.
- Although change is happening at a high speed, it is also the slowest it will ever be.
- The pace will continue to be relentless, there is less context to make decision, we have new expectations and society is changing.
- The next decade will be the most disruptive in human history.

Interestingly the stats are that apparently the economic potential of Gen AI is \$2.6-4.4T. However, how will that new wealth be distributed? Hopefully, it will be reflected in all salaries within all companies, including the supply chains, but this will require legislation and bold leaders.

We need to approach and think of change differently – we need to disrupt ourselves. As we approach this "new renaissance age," we need to be more like a renaissance leader. Now by definition this predominately sums up to be a master of all things. However, that is not very helpful in today's world. So instead, let's use it in the sense of being willing to explore ideas from all the different areas, rather than immediately dismissing some and only exploring a limited view. The skills of a renaissance leader are:

- Open-minded.
- Self-aware.
- Willing to unlearn.
- Bring diverse opinions together to tackle challenges.
- Trust their people.
- Value people's gifts and talents.
- Collaborate rather than command and control.

We need to lift our heads up from the micro details and start asking and answering the right questions and stop putting barriers on imagination. It is about being willing to unlearn things and that includes our automatic mindset of judging first, explore later. We need to have a diverse group of people around us from not just diverse backgrounds, but also diverse perspectives and areas of "expertise" to help us potentially view and approach a challenge in a different way (Bryan 2024a).

For example, everyone experiences change, whether they like it or not – it happens in everyone's life and we know it is going to continue to happen rapidly over the next 10 years. So, why not ask a painter about their experience with change and how they prefer or would have preferred it be done– or a dancer, or a graduate, or a financial person, or an environmentalist, etc. Now you may not get exactly what you think you might need from all those conversations, but you never know – creativity and open-mindedness enable more creativity and innovation. Exploring a subject from a completely different perspective can create opportunities and solutions that you would never have thought of before (Bryan 2024a).

And that is what it means to be a renaissance leader. Saying "hmmm" more and "no" less. It is about asking questions that perhaps no one else is asking. It is about saying "what if" and "why/why not" and exploring the possibilities with others. Sharing ideas and discussing them rather than telling people what to do and feeling like you have all the answers because you don't and nor should you. It is not about you, it is about the collective of all the people.

When we talk about organisational change and transformation, we are talking about a large collective of people in which change will impact, so it only makes sense to have them involved from the beginning with the change.

Asking them questions to see if this is even the right type of change or the right time for the change. It is about exploring more and controlling less (Bryan 2024a).

There will be times when things don't go well, and/or throw us for a loop, because let's face it, the best plans do not always go according to plan, and that is ok. So, instead of getting scared or upset or paralysed to make a decision, let's shout – plot twist – and have fun with the creativity and innovation we will draw upon to manage the situation. Afterall, "Creativity is intelligence having fun."

I was working for an infrastructure organisation when a construction programme was going very wrong in Monaco. The developer, architect and project management firms had been at constant loggerheads for quite a period of time which was starting to have major ramifications on the actual development of the new buildings. As a result, it was decided that a workshop would be delivered to help bring the three different teams together into one room to work through not just the construction challenges but also start to understand how their different working styles were impacting on other people and how they did things. Now one of the challenges in delivering this workshop was that it needed to be delivered entirely in French, as there was one person on one of the teams who amazingly spoke four languages, but unfortunately for me, none were English. So, two people who spoke fluent French and had the technical skills to deliver the workshop were sent in; however, neither of these individuals had the behavioural understanding that was also needed. So I was sent in, even though my skill level in French was extortionately low – at best could be called "Fronglais." In any case, we all went down and I tried my best to communicate, when needed, drawing up my high school French, as best I could. At one point though, in the middle of one of the days of the workshop, I noticed some alarming behaviour – I must confess, I had absolutely NO IDEA what was being said by anyone in the room, but I immediately walked up to the facilitator at the front of the room, turned my back from the audience and told her to call a break right now. She then said they were in the middle of something, but I insisted and said I don't care whatever is going on, but make an excuse and call a break NOW. Otherwise, this person is going to pick up his chair and throw it across the room at that person. Needless to say, she promptly called a break and the said person could not have leapt out of their chair and left the room fast enough.

The facilitator asked me how did I know what was going on and I said, I could see the veins in his neck throbbing and the colour in his face turning and knew there was a major problem.

After the break, the person returned to the room and things were able to be carried on without issue. The point of this story is that we need to take time to notice what all is going on around us and as leaders this is extremely important. We can only do this if we take the time to stop, breathe and listen, so we can see how others are feeling and being impacted.

Key points

- Enabling change requires the involvement of people because mindsets and behaviours will need to change.
- Stop, breathe and listen are the three most important things a leader can do.
- Need to ask the question, "how else can this be done."
- Disrupt yourself and be more of a renaissance leader.

Key questions

1. What can you do to be more people focus?
2. What are your biggest challenges in your organisation?
3. How can you incorporate the renaissance leadership skills into your practice?

3

CREATING PSYCHOLOGICAL SAFETY

Communication planning begins with careful analysis of the audiences, key messages and the timing for those messages.

Tim Creasey and Jeffrey Hiatt

Change can be nerve-racking, exciting, stressful, scary and fun. The key is to approach change as an opportunity to explore and experience something different. After all, many of you reading this probably go on a different holiday each year, right? So, the trick is to bring that same approach to change we have many times in our personal lives into our professional lives.

Can we plan for everything or know exactly what is going to happen at each moment – of course not. That is part of the experience though, and is what many times makes it exciting as well as scary. Before I was married and had kids, a couple times a year, I would either take my car or rent one and go to a map, close my eyes and pick a place with my finger and

DOI: 10.4324/9781003643692-3

decide to go there. Sometimes I ended up at the place my finger randomly chose and sometimes I would be on the road, see something and decide to stop and go there instead. I had no idea what was going to happen at each moment, or did I know where I would always end up. In some ways, this was a little scary, but it was also really exciting and I ended up in some amazing places with great experiences I would not have had otherwise.

When we are leading change, it is critical to understand the people who we anticipate to actually do the change. Now this may sound obvious, but the number of times a project team gets so involved in the project and focused on the things that need to get done, that they forget about the people, whose help they will need to actually enable the change to happen is incredible.

Building trust

When we ask ourselves what it takes to help people through change and lead, the one skill that is repeated over and over again is **trust**. But what is trust really and how do we know we have it? Who do we need to have it with? According to the Oxford dictionary, "trust is to believe that somebody is good, honest, sincere, etc. and that they will do what you expect of them or do the right thing" (2023). To be honest (no pun intended), this sounds very subjective – how do we know someone is good, honest and sincere? This is down to belief – we believe someone to be these things and we base that belief on seeing the person doing what we expect of them, i.e. they said they would do x and then they did x and hence what we would expect. This then follows on the research that was conducted by the Chartered Institute for Personnel Development (CIPD) back in 2012 that outlined the requirements that it takes to build trust, calling it "The Pillars of Trust," which entails four attributes an individual needs:

- Ability to be perceived as leading – how do people know you are leading? How do you know people are seeing you as a leader?
- Benevolence for others – how are you showing others you care and have concern for their well-being, as a human?
- Integrity – how are you demonstrating your honesty and values?
- Predictability – how are you being consistent in what you do?

So, what does this mean in regard to the types of behaviours a leader will need to help people through change? Being perceived as having an ability to do something means there is a degree of confidence demonstrated. There is also a degree of capability and technical understanding. In leadership terms, this can be demonstrated through emotional intelligence which links directly to being able to demonstrate a level of care and concern for staff (benevolence). When it comes to enforcing the rules, it is done consistently and equally across all staff to demonstrate fairness with a sharing of the knowledge and process of the decision-making (integrity and predictability). Now this is not to say that leaders need to be able to predict the future, but it is to say that regardless of what happens in the future, their behaviour, based on their integrity, could be foreseen in how they will manage and lead in any given situation.

Now you may be starting to think, this all sounds reasonable, but so what? What does this all have to do with leading people in change? And the simple answer is this – as leaders of change, we need to be demonstrating a care for others, rather than just bulldoze a change into an organisation (Elon Musk's Twitter, now X, takeover, immediately springs to mind). It is not to say that change won't happen if we do it this way, in some shape or form, but the cost could be too high and the return on investment will definitely be quite low, as a result.

Brene Brown defines trust using the acronym "braving" (2020). This is based on boundaries being respected and clear, reliability in you doing what you say you will do, accountability for your mistakes, vault meaning you don't share information or experiences that are not yours, integrity (which will come up again later on) in regards to you choosing what is right rather than what is fun/fast or easy, nonjudgement when someone comes to you with a request or thought or feeling, and finally generosity in your intentions, words and actions of others (Brown 2020).

We also need to demonstrate consistency in our behaviours, not to say and do and treat everything exactly the same, but we are consistent in our approach, and if there is a change, we articulate why we have decided to do things differently in that instance. This is the same as we would act in our personal lives – if typically we plan and book our holidays in advance and then suddenly book one last minute, we would articulate why we did this on this occasion – we needed a break because…. Or I wanted to be spontaneous and surprise….

Looking after our people

The point is, the more of the human elements, i.e. people centric, we use when we are leading people in change, the greater the level of success because our teams will see us as the person we are and how we are trying to look after them, as best we can. To do this, the first three questions we should seek to be able to answer, as we will have to give people this information to help them on the change are:

1. What is driving the change?
2. Why now? Why not 6 months ago or in 6 months' time?
3. How do people think/feel about it? Are they supercharged and desperate for it, think it is a nice to have to could care less and see it as a waste of time?

Knowing the answers to these questions will determine the tone, style and approach to the change along with the communications, and are the first questions I ask any potential client, before embarking on anything.

An infrastructure company was going through a large complex and complete digital transformation programme. After 9 months, there was a general feeling of frustration amongst the senior project/workstream leads that people were not taking on board and using a host of the different systems, processes, procedures that had been created. After hearing about this for a couple of days, I said, "This all sounds great and really amazing, buy why should 'Marie' in Brazil care about this?" (Marie being used as the name of an avatar I created). They all looked at me and started to give me what I would call "the management spiel of the efficiencies and effectiveness this would bring to Marie. So, again, I said "Yeah, so what? Why should Marie care about this, what makes this so important for her and does she know why this is important for her specifically?" That is when the penny dropped and the team realised they had not defined what the change was practically, much less the why it was needed and what people needed to do differently and why they needed to do it. People are curious creatures by nature and we like to explore different things, places, etc. However, in order for us to explore and get curious, we need an impetus – a reason. Just telling someone they have to do something or do what they have always done differently won't work (try telling a 2-year-old to do something without an explanation – this behaviour is ingrained in us).

Changing our approach made a great impact practically in a challenging area that meant we were able to achieve our objective.

(Russell 2018)

What is driving the change will pull out the why the organisation is
investing in the change in the first place. The answer should articulate the
"so what," what is the purpose of the change, and this needs to be beyond,
what I call, the management spiel of effectiveness and efficiencies. The
answer needs to get to the heart of the change – is it because the old system
is dead tech and hence has to be replaced? Is it because this will keep us
ahead of our competitors or the market? Is it because we want to {fill in the
blank}. That needs to be clearly articulated so people know what and why
they are doing this change – it gives them a vision to hold onto (more of
that in Chapter 4).

The next question of why now defines why the change needs to happen
in this timeframe versus another one that has already either passed or is
in the future. This helps people understand the need that much more and
prioritises it on their own "to-do" lists, which is important, as you will
need to elicit their help in achieving the change. So if this is not articulated
well, then it is difficult to get anyone to put the change at a high level of
their priorities and as a result it will end up at the bottom, which will not
necessarily be helpful for you.

The last question of what people think/feel about it – well this really
helps determine the tone of the messaging and the approach. If you know
people are not going to like the change for whatever the reasons, then you
will need to adjust the tone and approach differently than if you know
everyone is desperate for it and can't wait for it to happen.

I was working with one of my clients on a technology change, and
before I came on board, it was determined there was a fear of technology
in large parts of the organisation. However, when I observed one of the
first pilot sessions, I uncovered there was not a fear of technology but a
phobia, as the individuals in the room did not even want to touch the new
devices and turn them on. In fact, many voiced how they wished they
could have their fax machines back.

A phobia and a fear of something are very different, and the best way
I could relate to try and solve the problem was to think of my own phobia –
rats. There is a whole poltergeist reason for this, which I won't go into
now, but rest assured, if I were in their office and there were a rat in one

of the meeting rooms, there is absolutely no way I would go on that floor much less be any closer to it. And that is how these staff members felt about the new devices and software that were the start of the change. So, then I thought, what would it take for me to eventually get comfortable with a rat being in a meeting room? Long story short, a great deal of time to get use to the fact and allow the rat in my head to become wallpaper in the office. So, that is what I started to work on doing to solve the technology phobia for the staff. I knew there was an IT person either in each office all the time or at least part of the time in a week and they had a dedicated desk, as they were the on-hand technicians. I convinced the team to put a new device on the desk of every IT person straight away and make sure their desk was in a high traffic area – that way when the staff with the phobia walked by they would see it, and although they would not go near it at first, eventually over time they would. The aim was that by the time the staff received their new devices and software, they felt more comfortable with it because it was not entirely new to them.

Identifying how people feel in a 3D and virtual world

Understanding the thoughts and feelings of people – what is going on for them right now and how they might feel about the change is critical in creating psychological safety. The reason for this phobia was due to the fact that the staff members worked with the public at a time that was quite challenging for the public member. As a result, coding was used on various files outlining if that person had been violent in the past or verbally abusive, etc. The phobia stemmed from the fact that when the staff member was working with that public member and if they were prone to violence they would not necessarily be understanding and empathetic to the staff member if they "did something wrong" and had to quickly correct it. So, the phobia stemmed from a real fear of the staff members' safety.

So this begs the question, how can we find out what people are thinking and feeling? What clues can we pick up to get some indication how people are, so we can put forward the right messages, subliminal or otherwise, to obtain that initial positive moment?

We could study and use psychometrics to help us but that takes a good deal of investment to study and hence is not always possible or desirable when we are looking to find answers sooner rather than later. There is a method though we can all do, even a child.

We can start noticing the little clues people give us all the time. Have you ever gone to a café and people watched, and as you are watching start to make assumptions or stories in your head or maybe even share these ideas with a companion? If you haven't, then head to a café where there are multiple people pronto, as this is a great skill to develop.

Now this is all sounding good and we are starting to build our tactics and plans together, but the one area we have not tackled yet is understanding how we can communicate in a hybrid/virtual world. Now some of you may be thinking – well we all have to be back in the office full time, or we are completely remote. Whichever the case may be, whether you recognise/like or realise it, we are all living in a hybrid world. For the most part, not all of our teams are located in the same place in the world, we are also not always in the office or out of the office. There are times we do get together, whether it be only monthly or annually, there are moments. So understanding what the positives and negatives of communicating, leading and managing the f2f and virtual world will help us understand what we need to do not just leaders of change but leaders of people centric change. Why? Because we want our organisation to be one of the surviving 25% and we know to do that we need to demonstrate people-centric behaviours as leaders and managers of people, particularly in change.

Now some of you may ask, is this different to what we "usually" do and we can reflect back on the pandemic, the level of mental health increase, to realise, it is not only different, but many of us may struggle how to actually do it in a way to ensure we maintain the "people perspective."

How we show up on screen has changed from being superficial to a critical competence for human connection. Video technology has changed the social and aural cues we give and receive from each other.

When you are watching people in an organisation, you don't necessarily have the ability, particularly in a hybrid environment, to "watch" people like you do in a café. However, you can start to notice what behaviours people are exhibiting in meetings, with certain people, in certain situations. You can also notice what is and is not being said in chat platforms, emails, meetings, and other internal social areas. You can also get a sense as to what people might potentially be thinking and feeling from news in the media. For example, if there is an energy crisis or a war or a head of state election, then the "feeling/thoughts/perspectives" of people in general is many times discussed. And remember, the people in your organisation are also people in this society that is being discussed in the news;

so these external factors may influence how they behave, think and feel about the change you are planning. This will be discussed in more detail, later on in the book. The main point at this stage is to start to notice what is going on in and out of the organisation.

Once you have done this, then you can start to use the complexity learning cycle in which you start to interpret what you have noticed and identify any potential patterns (Varney 2021). Then you can decide best how to respond to what you have noticed, which contributes to building the potential approach to change.

Nowadays, we can see each other online, but we are still learning to **feel** each other. With the phone, we became skilled over time at paying attention to the physical cues present in the voice. With the advent of video image, you would think this would be easier, but we might have moved backwards in terms of our attention to embodied cues – we perhaps are distracted by the visual and wind up paying less attention potentially, than we might if we were face to face (Bryan and Higgins 2022). How many times have you been on a video call and either people do not have the camera on, or they do and you can see they are typing away. I have even seen this happen in face-to-face meetings sometimes, and it is obvious they are not just taking digital notes.

Workplaces have stumbled into this new video-mediated, hybrid world – often too busy to step back and look at what the practical implications are for managers and employees, preferring instead to hanker after some return to something like the old days or assume that the technology can be deployed without attention to the social norms that will make it a heaven or hell (or somewhere in between).

So, what do we as leaders of change need to do? The first thing is let go of any fantasy that there is some model, roped in, answer out there – we are not only at a time of experimentation and flux, but the answer will be determined more by what type of organisation do we want to be (more Chapter 4). As a result, what will work for one organisation or specific groups in specific situations will be different and there may need to be different solutions across the whole organisation.

So, an agile mindset is needed, not just in terms of being flexible in "doing change" but in one's orientation to people and their moods and feelings and how what was going on in the world shaped their emotional world, which we have already discussed.

As we have said before, as leaders we need to understand the pulse of what is happening in our teams and are aware of the impact of what is going on in the world, and then adjust what is going on in the business to fit the changing emotional landscape of the world (remember those external and internal influencing factors). Now that may be starting to sound easy, but the reality might feel a bit daunting, so taking a look at the positives and negatives of the f2f and virtual world might help give us some clues as to what we need to start to do, based on the culture and preferences within our organisation. I am willing to gamble though that it will be a little of both in the end in today's interconnected world. The choice between f2f and virtual will largely depend on the context, goals as well as the preferences of individuals and organisations (see Table 3.1 for details).

Social isolation is not something managers have felt to be part of their responsibility. However good or bad, coming into an office or workplace gives many people a visceral experience of social connection, of belonging

Table 3.1 Pros and cons of different types of interaction

	Positives	Negatives
Face to Face	Non-verbal communication is easier to pick up Easier to build relationships and personal connection Obtain immediate feedback based on the responses and reactions of people Resolve conflict easier to the reading of emotions and engagement High engagement as more people do not "multi-task" in the meeting Tailor messages more easily Increase in serendipity and unplanned interactions Increase personal impact Build trust and higher unity amongst team members	Geographical constraints Time and travel lead to more stress and higher costs Higher scheduling challenges Reduced flexibility Limited reach Resource intensive Inefficiencies as f2f meetings can become lengthy Limited recording/documentation Difficult to scale Generate exclusivity to those who can attend

(Continued)

Table 3.1 Continued

	Positives	Negatives
Virtual	Global Reach – not limited to geographical boundaries and hence can increase collaboration Cost savings – people don't need to travel, and overhead costs can be reduced Flexibility – work/life balance but also in response to customer/client needs as there aren't the restrictions of 9-5 Convenience – without the need for physical presence, it can make it easier to attend Reduced commute which can generate less stress Talent Pool Access – expanding the location allows the expansion of the talent Reduced carbon footprint Ability to record and document Inclusivity – minimise dominance of in-person dynamics Increase learning opportunities through webinars and virtual events	Isolation Data security Misinterpretations of non-verbal cues Technology glitches can create communication barriers Lack of balance between virtual and in-person interactions Difficult in building relationships and rapport Lack of work/life balance as the boundaries can be blurred Time zone challenges – if a message is delivered at the "right" time in one zone but not in the other and/or one receiving the message before another can create a feeling of "not a priority" Limited engagement as people may not participate fully and hence disengage Cultural differences can be amplified if messages are not tailored Lack of immediate feedback as people may not feel able or hesitant to speak in a large virtual setting Reduced serendipity/ spontaneous interactions Difficult to deal with conflicts

to a community – which is an essential need for the social mammal that we are. Without that sense of connection, people will usually suffer psychologically and, from an organisational perspective, measures such as reported loyalty, trust and commitment may take a hit.

Managers now have to learn how to pay attention to experiences such as loneliness and isolation to a much greater extent than they have historically, which is not something many will feel equipped for. But how can we know what is having an impact on teams and individuals? What is constraining their liveliness? It's not just a matter of asking people, although that's often an overlooked first step, it's also about noticing what people are NOT saying as much as what they are saying. It's about lifting our heads as leaders up from just thinking about the next things on our to-do list and really seeing what is being shared with us – reading the liveliness in the room, be that on- or offline.

Even the least socially skilled manager or employee is wired to pick up what others are experiencing when people are physically together (whether they choose to act on what they're picking up is another matter!). In the online world, people need to pay much closer attention to the cues that people are giving each other – or to become more explicit in stating what is going on for them, much as in a phone call, people may ask others to say what their silence means when there is a pause in the conversation.

If there is a "special ingredient" for leading change that is integrity, a word and concept used in business without any real understanding of what it means beyond some bland statements, or a simplistic appeal to fiduciary or other legal duty (Bryan and Higgins 2023). The Oxford dictionary defines integrity as meaning "the quality of being honest and having strong moral principles." But what does it really mean to be honest and have strong moral principles in business? At a time, when people's distrust of organisations is at such a high level, the question of integrity and honesty is paramount, particularly in change. All the communication and influencing skills in the world could be present, but if people don't have faith in the integrity of leaders and managers, and the integrity of the interests served by those with power, then change leadership will just be another one of those organisational rituals that generate a lot of heat and not much light. Or worse further fuel cynicism and disengagement (Bryan and Higgins 2023).

However, a focus on integrity is not of itself enough; there is also the need for leaders to be emotionally mature and sophisticated because leading people through change is an emotional experience – it gets to the guts of human emotions because there will be difficult conversations, established relationships will be broken and new ones needed. Telling people that what they want is not going to happen is never easy, or that the secure job they were anticipating – and underpinned their mortgage application – is now up for grabs and the security they hoped for is no longer there (Bryan and Higgins 2023).

Recognising that everyone is, to varying degrees, outside of their comfort zone is needed when reviewing and understanding how to build sustainable and resilient change in organisations – in other words, understanding the situation from other people's perspective, regardless of your position, is critical.

I was working for an infrastructure company and the Managing Director and executive sponsor of the change was at the printer/photocopy machine, which was not far from the tea/coffee point in the office. I was in the area with a colleague who had a document they were looking to photocopy, so decided, as it was being used, to make a cup of coffee. The Managing Director then turned to her and asked if she was looking to make some copies of the document, to which she replied positively. He then promptly said I will do it for you – how many copies do you want? This very simple and honest act of kindness clearly illustrated a level of benevolence and integrity from the top leadership position role modelling the type of behaviour that was widely demonstrated across the business.

In complete contrast to that, at a public sector organisation, the top leadership actually demonstrated a level of bullying and disrespect for those who worked "underneath them," which again meant that this behaviour was replicated at different levels, making the workplace quite toxic. I experienced this once when I was called in to do a "change deep dive" which typically involves pulling together all the different activities and engagements that had been done to date and what is planned in the middle of a programme. This is not unusual because the trick with people change, when done well, is that it is happening in a multitude of places in regard to different communications, engagements, training and activities. As a result, usually two weeks are given to pull everything together. In this scenario, I was given 24 hours, which should have alerted me of what was to come. In all honesty, I could have given a presentation on funny cats, for all the difference it would have made. Instead, I did manage to pull together what had been achieved in the 8 weeks upon receiving approval of the strategy and plans. One of the key achievements was the fact that I had a team in place, which was not the situation beforehand, and so I also brought the team in the meeting with me to introduce them to the executive sponsors. Needless to say, we received a major kicking that was disrespectful, unwarranted and unjustified. The best way I could describe it was we walked into a gun fight with a bag of candy. After that meeting, one of my team members, who had only been at the organisation for 1 week at the time, received another offer elsewhere and obviously took it and promptly resigned. This person had a simple choice to make: either go somewhere where they knew, based on previous experience, would be respected and valued vs the current place where they felt they would not – the choice was obvious.

What we do and how we do things as leaders can make all the difference in the world. People will vote with their feet, when it comes to a workplace. So, if you want your organisation to be productive and successful, particularly in change, you need to understand what is going on with people and how are they being impacted.

Key points

- Building trust requires integrity, compassion, perception of leading and predictability.
- Leading change goes beyond just empathy – it is about finding out how people think and feel.
- Notice what is going on in the organisation – how people are thinking and feeling about life, much less the organisation and potentially the change.
- There is no one size fits all for communicating and engaging in the workplace, much less change.
- There are positives and negatives to virtual and f2f activities.
- If there is one key ingredient to leading change, it is integrity.

Reflective questions

1. Before you go get Board/budget approval for your change, ask yourself the three questions:
   - What is ultimately driving the change?
   - Why now?
   - How will the people feel about it?
2. What have you noticed going on around your organisation? What are people saying/doing and what are they not saying/doing?
3. What is the difference you want people to do as a result of the change? How is that different to the current state?

4

SUSTAINABLE CHANGE

All change is people change.

Dex Hunter Torricke

We talked earlier about the analogy of change being a story or journey and one of the key questions being, what story do you want to share. The reason the word share is used deliberately is because change is not a one man band activity. So how do we create a vision for change and how do you do this so we build resilience in our organisations and people, as well as make the change people centric?

It is fascinating how we can take many lessons from different areas of life and apply them in business. For example, I was watching a modern ballet dance that used rope in the movement. The relationship of the dancers, the mood, the emotion were all defined by this use of the rope. Then towards the end, the ropes were taken away and everything changed – the performers were liberated, unconstrained. At first like a frenzy, but then the dancers started to gel together letting go of the need for the rope to keep things together/working in harmony.

DOI: 10.4324/9781003643692-4

This created an analogy in my head for leading change and raises the question, what are the constraints, the "ropes," of organisational change?

Before we answer this question, we need to uncover what makes up or rather is organisational change? Big question, and there are a number of different philosophies out there and we could literally write multiple books on this subject (and hence many already exist), but we aren't here to make things more complicated. The purpose of this book is to give a practical guide for managers and leaders in how best to lead people in change. So, if we look at the very basic definition of change being the process of going from one state to another state (Lewin 1935) and organisational change as the process of an organisation going through that simple transition, then the next logical question is how? We all know change is not that simple, but yet we do sometimes make it more complicated than it really needs to be, as we discussed earlier.

When we are looking at implementing a change, we want it to last and be sustainable because that is one of the key elements of obtaining a high level of our return of investment (discuss more later) – as change should always be seen as an investment, not a cost. If you are looking at it as a cost, then why are you doing it?

Sustainable change

So how do you create a sustainable change? Sustainable change is based on two elements – the level of activity and level of engagement. Referring to the matrix (Figure 4.1), to create sustainable change, there needs to be a high level of engagement and activity with people going in the same direction. People need to be actively motivated and participate in the activities involved consistently and regularly that promote, encourage and embody the change required. If there is a high level of engagement but a low level of activity, then there is a risk of generating a frenzy of highly motivated people but with no focus or shared direction to engage their motivations. This can lead to frustration, disillusionment and cynicism with the change. If there is high activity but low engagement, then there ends up being a great deal happening but no one is either aware of the activity or is inclined to actually get involved. This de-prioritises the change and ultimately leads to the change not happening – all talk no action many times ends up being the mantra describing that change. If there is no engagement and no activity,

Figure 4.1 Sustainable change.

then the change is at a stalemate and ultimately gets forgotten about and seen as either an empty promise or inconsequential organisational rhetoric.

When I was working with a chemicals and sustainable technology company, they had a definitive and ambitious vision that completely focused on creating a sustainable world. The vision really invoked inspiration and motivation in people. As a result, there were a number of different activities going on with the vision in mind in multiple parts of the business – in many ways, it was quite inspiring, but none of them were coordinated or linked with any other activity/initiative or another part of the business. As a result, it meant that once the activities were done in one area, they disappeared and were not repeated in other areas, regardless of their success in that one distinct business area. This then prompted a group of people to start off a coordination of the vision across different business areas. However, there was very little activity, which meant that the highly motivated individuals in the group were running around in a frenzy thinking they are coordinating the vision across the business but without activity to actually coordinate. This led to people feeling disenfranchised and thinking the business was not really supporting the vision, in the manner in which they understood it. A solution was to bring all this together and create an overarching coordinated plan and roadmap, which required uncovering all the amazing work being done in multiple different places by and with multiple different people. This can take a good deal of time, but it is possible. The challenge is once this has been achieved and the activities are illustrated into one document, it can sometimes feel overwhelming for the audience to realise just how much activity is actually already happening. However, having this information is invaluable because it allows the people of the organisation to give the activities a purpose that is coordinated and linked to the organisational vision.

So that all sounds like reasonable theory, but how do we create a high level of engagement and activity. To begin, there needs to be a common vision for all to follow because this gives everyone a clear direction and path.

Visioning

The first thing we need to decide is where we are trying to get to – what is it we are trying to achieve? What is the ultimate aim/goal and hence vision? In the simplest of terms, what do we want?

To start from an organisational transformation perspective, we need to clear our minds of the here and now and think of the world in 10 years' time. Why so long down the road, because that gives us the flexibility to be creative – really creative. The world is your oyster because 10 years is a long way off, so given free rein, what do you want? What kind of an organisation do you want to be? How do you want to be thought of and perceived? How do you want to think and feel about the organisation and how do you want your teams to feel, your clients and customers, the market place and industry? Visualise that desire and write it down and be specific with it. Visions that say "to be the market leader in xyz industry" are not specific and don't mean anything – what does it mean to be a market leader? No one really knows, so be specific. A vision that is an action statement is a powerful and specific way to galvanise others to act and hence generate sustainable and resilient organisational change. So make your vision an action statement. Several companies have done this:

Microsoft: "to help people and businesses throughout the world realize their full potential." (https://www.microsoft.com/en-gb/about/)
Johnson Matthey: "to create a cleaner and healthier world." (https://matthey.com/careers/life-at-jm#:~:text=purposeful,restoring%20hearing%20or%20boosting%20crops)

Mott MacDonald: "to improve society by considering social outcomes in everything we do." (https://www.mottmac.com/about-us/delivering-on-our-purpose)

That is just to name a few – you can find more on the Internet yourself. The point is that each of the above statements has an action to it. This enables the people inside the business to know what they need to do to contribute to the vision and also is a clear statement to the market, clients and customers what the organisation is trying to achieve in their actions. Other people can visualise helping others achieve their full potential or a cleaner/healthier world or consider social outcomes. Now don't get me wrong, how the actual vision that all these different people envision will not be the same, but that is ok – the point is they know what they are trying to create when they work for the company and do whatever it is they are doing, thus creating a common goal and direction for everyone to follow.

An infrastructure company was embarking on multiple changes across the organisation, but there was one that had been going on for over a year and they had spent millions of pounds on all the changes there were creating within this programme. However, upon reading all the literature and programme documents, there were a great deal of objectives and key milestones articulated, but there was no vision. They had no idea what the ultimate aim of the change programme was and hence could not begin to help others onto the journey, communicate, train or anything because they did not know where they were going, much less when they would get there, or what or why they were ultimately trying to achieve. As a result, they had to go through a whole visioning exercise which made them real-ise the scope of the programme was much greater than just the project team and required restructuring the leadership, budget and programme itself.

To help achieve the vision, we need to be able to plan in a short- medium- long-term arena – technically this is called horizon scanning (Gates 1995), but practically it is about creating goals/objectives at a high level to help achieve the greater vision. It is best to define these areas by working backwards from the vision. For example, if you know what your vision is and it has been defined clearly with an action statement, then you can start to identify what is it that needs to happen just before you achieve the vision, which are then the long-term goals. After that, you can then identify what needs to happen just before you get to the long-term goals and that becomes the medium term. Finally, you can then identify what needs to happen just before the medium-term goals and that becomes your short term. Going through this process really helps then identify exactly what needs to happen to get started on the journey of making the vision a reality.

These techniques make visioning practical and can help organisations decide what are the priorities and where should resources be invested to create the greatest impact. This also enables a degree of flexibility for leaders to plan for the future, whilst being adaptable to uncertainty and unforeseen circumstances that will inevitably occur during the 10-year vision journey. (This can also be used for individual development at any career level to help you, as a person, make intentional decisions regarding your own professional and personal life.)

Once you have done this, do not immediately go out and communicate it to the world – remember, change, and particularly organisational change, is not a one man band activity, so just because you have created a vision with long-, medium- and short-term goals does not mean it is the right vision. You need to sit on it for a whilst and test out the potential concept by starting to use the holistic approach (which is laid out in the next chapter).

Furthermore, creating a vision that is far into the future and using the holistic approach builds the ability to deal with the uncertainty that will inevitably occur by enabling clear decision-making. If the disruption takes the organisation further away from the vision and the organisation still believes the vision is the right direction, then decisions can be made to manage the disruption with the aim of getting back to the vision. Whereas, if it is then decided the vision, as a result, is no longer valid, then decisions can be made taking all that into consideration and develop a new vision that will be more appropriate.

I have used this same method on a personal and career development arena for myself and for others. A friend of mine was at a point in her career where she knew she wanted something slightly different, but was unsure of what that was exactly, much less how to even get there. So we used the above visioning exercise to help build a career plan for her. First, I had her imagine, if the world was her oyster and there were absolutely no obstacles or financial constraints, what would she be doing and how in 10 years' time. At first, she giggled, and then when she realised I was serious, she took quite some reflection time. Her initial response contained barriers, so I reinforced the possibility there were no barriers or financial constraints. It was then that she started to really dream and visualise and completely different future for herself. Upon further digging and definition, after not too long, she had a very clear vision of herself and what her life could genuinely be in 10 years. Now the question was how does she get there. So, we immediately started to work backwards, first looking at the actions that needed to happen immediately before the vision was achieved to create the long-term goals; then we did this again to create the medium term and then finally again for the short term. There was some tweaking along the way in the plan to ensure its validity, but after some time, I was able to ask and she was able to answer what is it that she needed to do now to get started.

We completed this exercise just over 2 years ago, and recently she has been thrown a disruptor, a redundancy from her current job. However, as she had a clear plan at this point in place and had been actively delivering this plan, she was able to immediately go back to it and see how she needed to amend it, just slightly, to take into consideration of the new situation. To her surprise, the redundancy was not as "bad" of a change scenario as she first felt – she was able to quickly realise that due to the change in circumstances, it only meant that some things she had planned slightly later on down the road could come into play sooner. She was able to make the decision as to whether she tries to replicate her current circumstances and find a "new permanent job" or catapult some other options identified later into now, giving her a clear decision-making power. At a turbulent and emotional time, this gave her the confidence and empowerment to make the best decision for her and her family, which she felt she would not have been able to do, nearly as positively and clearly, had she not had the vision and plan already mapped out.

Key points

- Change is emotional, so we need to treat everyone as humans not robots.
- What story do you want to share?
- For great impact on the organisation, the change needs to be sustainable and that requires a clear, actionable vision.

Reflective questions

1. What are you trying to achieve?
2. What do you want to be, as an organisation? How do you want to be perceived by yourselves and by others – clients, customers, teams, colleagues, peers, family, friends, etc.
3. How are you going to make your change sustainable?

5

HOLISTIC APPROACH TO CHANGE

Entrenched mental models will thwart change....

Peter M. Senge

Both leadership and change are contested labels and there is no universal definition. What is usefully understood by leadership and change is specific to the unique nature of a particular change and the evolving context within which it is being carried out. By paying attention to what is specifically needed in the moment around leaders and leading, change leadership becomes an approach that is fit for a specific purpose and avoids becoming a generic approach which is incapable of adjusting to local realities. By noticing how the context of change is evolving and assumptions become validated and invalidated, so the fitness of the chosen approach is also kept under constant review.

(Bryan and Higgins 2023)

What is a holistic approach? It means all encompassing – where we take into consideration the potential external and internal influencing factors,

DOI: 10.4324/9781003643692-5

the hard and soft not just on the vision/change itself but also on the business, which includes the industry and market. This creates the context for change and the circumstances that need to be considered in the planning stage. There needs to be an analysis to obtain an understanding of the potential enablers and hurdles in areas like industry regulation through to layers of company policy and customary practice. Furthermore, what happens when these constraints don't exist anymore? What's the impact on people tasked with leading change (Figure 5.1)?

We all have ropes that shape our organisational life – and new ropes are always appearing as new things happen in the world. How we show up is a critical competence for modern human connection, as much as learning to read became a competence when the printing press made the written word widely available. It requires different skills and a willingness to pay attention to inter-personal habits that most of us have been able to take for granted for much of our lives. To be a leader of change means learning how to tap into the collective experience of these ropes/constraints – and finding a way for people to step beyond them and into the relationships that give them the energy to embrace change. This includes setting boundaries, creating spaces and clearly illustrating listening techniques to help create the social interaction we all crave.

The world is very complex and multi-faceted with lots of different factors having impacts on organisational change, whether it be a small or large transformation.

Like the dancers, these things change our relationships, our mood and our feelings about the change. We need to review the potential these impacts have on us, as leaders, and our staff, particularly in relation to the change we are embarking, as this will greatly impact the level of

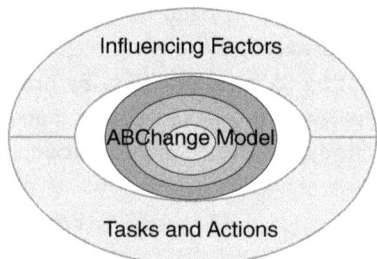

Figure 5.1 Holistic approach to change.

success our change will have on our organisation. Once we have done that, we then apply that influencing data to the ABChange framework to determine how best to lead people and from there create our plans for change.

That is the process, so let's look at this step by step.

Step 1: external influencing factors

One of the first tactics we can use is the tried a tested and very well-known PESTLE model (Aguilar 1967) to unpick the external factors. This includes the political dynamics within an organisation as well as outside – the war in Ukraine, Gaza Strip and Brexit, as well as the pandemic, has illustrated very clearly how governmental politics plays a big impact on all our lives in different ways, generating a variety of emotions and circumstances that are complex and difficult to manoeuvre, as a leader of an organisation. In addition, there are the economic fluctuations that follow these situations and the change in societal norms and expectations.

Now this may seem arbitrary and you may question why these external factors really matter and the simple answer is because they affect our lives – personally and professionally, as humans, and therefore will affect our change and our business. For example, when a country is going through an energy crisis or is thrown into war or legislation suddenly changes due to elections or change in government policy, can and does have major ramifications on the people. This then impacts the change, because how confident and secure people feel in life affects how confident and secure they feel about themselves and the work they do and hence how willing and sometimes able to accept or manage a change, regardless of how big or small or fabulous it may or may not be.

Step 2: internal influencing factors

The next step is to identify the internal influencing factors; again, like the external factors, they have an influence on how ready the organisation and people are to start on the change – what will help/hinder the change (remember the example earlier about the performance management process and the impact on a leader implementing people-centric change). So, to help us really define the internal influencing factors, we can use the organisational development approach defined in previous published works, but for ease we will recap here (Bryan 2021):

Business: What is the current and future business strategy and how will this change affect it? Will it change it completely? What is the organisation's commitment level? How will buy-in and commitment of the executive sponsor be obtained?

Culture: What is the culture of the organisation – will it help or hinder the change and how and why? What has happened historically in the organisation – has there been a number of restructures/large growth and has this been tried before?

Team: Is there a team of people that already exists to deliver the change or do they need to be brought in? How will the team be structured? What, if any, are the support structures/networks internally? What is the structure of the organisation and how deliverables completed – will this help or hinder the change?

Policies and Procedures: Will the existing systems and processes help or hinder the change? Do they need to change along with any policies or procedures? Will this impact any potential timelines within the change? Is there a budget, and how will this be managed?

Space: What is the environment in which this change is happening in the workplace – is it hybrid, completely remote? What do people need to make this change happen? Will the current spaces available help/hinder the change? Do different ones need to be created?

IT Capability: What are the current IT and HR systems and processes – will they help or hinder the change? Do they need to change in any way?

Once we have defined and analysed the external and internal influencing factors, we then start to build a picture of readiness for the organisation that brings the future context of change into focus. We can also start to answer some of the potential questions and challenges we may get when we start to share the vision/change with others.

Before we can move on however, we need to also take a look at the assumptions we have made in the first two steps with the external and internal influencing factors, as this can have a huge impact on our analysis results. For example, there was an engineering firm who were moving to cloud technology, and they went through this process. However, as they did so, they made the assumption that employees in all the regions would have "reasonable" access to the Internet, and it turned out this was not the case for several teams. Unfortunately this was picked up quite late and once the organisation made the move meaning that there were a couple of teams that did not have access for periods of time to company systems and processes creating a delay in the projects, which incurred additional costs.

Step 3: ABChange model

Once you analysed the external and internal influencing factors with the assumptions made along the way, you then use this information to define and obtain a real understanding of the type of change in which is being planned and the potential impacts it will have on the people and the organisation itself.

The next step is to ask what is at the root of this change – of what you are trying to achieve. The ABChange model (Figure 5.2) gives a clear direction

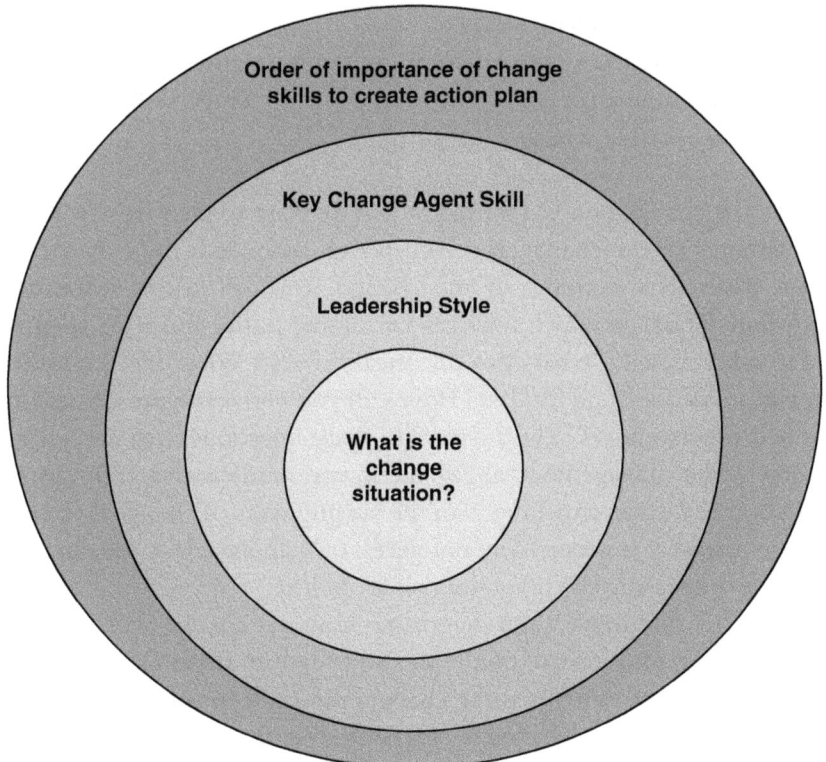

Figure 5.2 ABChange model.

on what is needed to lead the people of the organisation through a specific type of change, so it is critically important to identify the right type of change. Once you have identified the type of change, the leadership style and change skills are defined for you, and all that is left is for you to put into your specific context and definitions (after all, we all define things ever so slightly differently – what I think is a coaching leadership style, for example, may be slightly different to what you think.)

This is why it is really very important to identify the right type of change (Table 5.1). There are two pitfalls with the ABChange model that may people have fallen into:

1.   When they look at the table with all the details and leadership styles they say, "oh I like that leadership style, therefore it must be that type of change." Let me be extraordinarily clear when I say, IT IS NOT THE LEADERSHIP STYLE THAT DEFINES THE TYPE OF CHANGE YOU ARE DEALING WITH. IT IS THE TYPE OF CHANGE THAT DETERMINES THE CORRECT LEADERSHIP STYLE.
2.   If you focus 80% of your attention on the least important change skill outlined, rather than on the most important change skill, the change WILL go horribly wrong.

To make the change people focused, it is important to plan out the leadership elements of the change and incorporate them into the over-arching change plans. For example, if the change you are dealing with is an improvement change which requires a coaching leadership style, then you need to ask yourself, "what does this mean to you? What does a coaching leadership style look and feel like? How will you know you are doing it and how will others know?" The answers to these questions then are fed into the stakeholder management, engagement, communications, training, etc.

To not really understand and plan the leading tasks of change is to create a change plan that is generic and not necessarily applicable to the change at hand, thus increasing the potential risk for failure.

The factors that impact and determine how the change will affect our people and organisation are quite vast. So to ignore these elements is not only detrimental to our plans for change, but quite possibly catastrophic to the success. How the change is perceived, felt/thought about and experienced determines whether the change is viewed as an enemy or a friend.

Table 5.1 ABChange framework (2009)

Type of change situation	Leadership style	Most important skill	Other skills ranked by importance	Least important skill
Radical change	Visionary	Build trust	Collaboration, work across business functions, stake reward, self-confidence, respect change process	Work independently
Improvement	Coaching	Build trust	Collaboration, self-confidence, work across business units, stake reward, respect change process	Work independently
Healing discourse	Affiliative	Trust, self-confidence, collaboration	Work independently, stake reward, work across business units	Respect change process
Build buy-in consensus	Democratic	Trust, collaboration	Self-confidence, working across business units, respect change process, work independently	Stake reward
High performance, motivated team	Pace-Setting	Self-confidence	Build trust, work across business units, Collaboration, stake reward, respect change process	Work independently
Crisis, emergency	Commanding	Self-confidence	Work independently, collaboration, stake reward, build trust, work across business functions	Respect change process

This, in turn, has an impact on the level of potential survival of an organisation in a time where there is a great deal of uncertainty and complexity, which is only going to increase as time goes on. After all, we cannot plan for every eventuality, but we can prepare for managing uncertainty whilst we plan for the future to enable us and our organisation to thrive, rather than just survive change.

1. Use the holistic approach to change by defining the external and internal factors that will influence the organisation and the change.
2. Analyse the data to identify the type of change so there is clarity of the scale and impact of the change on the people and the organisation.
3. Use the ABChange framework to plan how best to lead people throughout the transformation, which includes the maintenance and adaptations of the change.
4. Create a high level of activity along with a high level of engagement to develop sustainability and flexibility to adapt to the changing needs and environments of the people and business.

Now that we know what it is we are trying to do and have considered all the potential implications that could influence the change and know what we as leaders need to do in regards to a leadership style and what that means, we now can start to take a look at how we are going to communicate this to people to obtain their buy-in/cooperation/help/guidance, etc.

Firstly, it is to recognise there is not a one size fits all or a simple answer. Change is an emotional process and experience, regardless of the type of change. So, it takes a level of emotional maturity to actually address, manage and lead in change. And yet the language used around change is typically rational and technocratic. At the same time, to address the emotion, many times the word passion is overused to such an extent that it loses its power, particularly with a large organisational transformation. Change gets to the guts of being human – there are difficult conversations to be had, and established relationships that may be broken or new ones needed (Bryan and Higgins 2023).

As a result of all that, a recognition that everyone is out of their comfort zone, albeit at varying degrees, and as a result a realisation that what people really need during these times is connection, feeling heard and cared about, i.e. feeling and believing they are understood.

Typically, many change projects and programmes start off either in the Board or Business Unit meeting room with an elite team of the usual suspects (and their usual advisers), trying to answer the question: "We need to do something to fix or improve or [insert verb] here." In doing so, the team members brainstorm or go away individually to think of "an answer," or what they might well think is THE answer, and then report back to the same group of people, and together they decide on not only what to do, but most of the time, how to do it as well. But rarely do they test this out with the people and get an understanding of the impact this may have on them, much less discover whether the answer is the "right" answer. And yet how valuable would that information be before embarking and investing a large amount of resources (people, systems and monies) into a change programme, especially if it ends up being the "wrong" answer.

In my experience, the best method is to use the end person in mind approach. What I mean by that is, you need to think about the person that is the furthest from the decision-making room and how they are going to first hear/discover/learn/gossip/find out about the project. What is going on for them and how might they react under certain circumstances? What is it that needs to be done that will help them "be ok" with the change when they first hear about it? If you can make their initial interaction with the change positive, then there is a high probability that everyone in between will have an initial positive experience too – thus tackling the first hurdle of change.

Most academic communication theories would talk about "knowing your audience" and the "end person in mind" approach utilises that theory but takes it to a whole new level so that we can understand what that is all about because it is about understanding the perspective from others and thinking about the "voice of the people." This can be done with surveys, focus groups, team briefings, townhalls – the list is endless. Just imagine, your leader came to you and said we were thinking of doing x, but wanted to know what you think before we decide that is what we are going to do – how valued, empowered, trustworthy you would feel. Now just imagine if you were that leader how much your staff and "most important asset, your people" would feel about you – that you took the time to ask them what they thought and genuinely asked, not just did it as a tick box exercise. The level of loyalty and pride people would feel and believe in you would be quite incredible.

Someone said to me the other day, "You don't [immediately] have to see the end of the staircase to take the first step," which is a good insight to remember. We are not "gurus of all information" and no one expects this of us really, but they do expect us to be human and treat people as people.

A technology firm was hired to help a public sector organisation implement a large digital transformation that affected 50,000 people. They shared how important it was to make sure the people element was done correctly, because they did a similar change for another public sector organisation and they did not involve the people and they were having to try to implement it a third time because it did not go well before and they did not want to repeat this situation. However, when they realised the time and effort it takes to obtain the "voice of the people," they wanted to shortcut things and not really involved the people, but instead only involved the existing IT team. Now considering the IT team were already bought into the project because they were helping with it, all the data they would receive would be a false positive, but it gave the appearance to the client they were involving the people. Unfortunately and predictably, when they rolled the change out to the wider teams, it did not go as planned and this cost the organisation a good deal in goodwill, productivity and money.

Change is an investment and needs to be treated as such – not a cost. It only becomes a cost when you don't maximise or optimise your ROI (return on investment). In your personal life, whenever you are going to spend money and/or time in your personal life, you determine the ROI on that activity. For example, when you think about going on a walk/run/gym session, the ROI is calculated based on how you will feel better and be more productive/healthy vs the time and/or money it costs. The ROI of meeting up with friends or family is calculated by the relationships that are valued getting stronger vs the time/money it will cost. With every activity from sleeping, eating, exercise, meeting up, shopping, holiday, personal time, etc., we automatically calculate our own personal ROI.

So why don't we do this in our business, particularly in change? ROI in change is calculated by assessing three different elements (Prosci 2016):

1. The speed of adoption – how quickly people have adopted the change and doing the "difference," whatever that difference is. In other words, how quickly are people demonstrating the new behaviours.

2. Utilisation of the change – how many people are demonstrating the new behaviours needed for the change.
3. Proficiency – how well are individuals performing in comparison to the level expected in the design of the change. How much has the dial changed in performance due to the change.

When I was working with a technology firm, I helped redevelop their entire workspace, which impacted on the staff working in a completely different way and thus changing their behaviours, relationships and interactions. Before we started the change though, we wanted to be able to track the ROI, so I set up four measurements:

1. The speed of adoption was going to be tracked based on how many people started to work in the office rather than elsewhere. Prior to the change, the space was a bit of a "chicken coop" with just rows and rows of assigned desks. This meant that if people did come into the office to work, many times they could be sitting completely by themselves because another person could be several rows away, thus devaluing the benefits of being in the office.
2. The utilisation of the change was measured through quantified observations on how people used and worked in the space – what space they used and for what purpose.
3. Proficiency was measured through sales targets – how the teams performed prior to the change in regard to sales vs after the change.
4. Satisfaction levels – I crafted a survey and delivered it before the change started to get a measurement on how they felt about the workspace vs how they felt about it afterwards.

Through very close understanding of the needs of the business, people's needs and feelings, along with managers requirements and feelings, I worked very closely with an interior designer and the project team to deliver a workplace that would not only enable more spaces for people to work in the exact same square footage, but give options to different types of working with an additional of biodiversity, colour and vibrancy. The results of which were startling and became quite the showpiece across the whole organisation. Teams that previously had decided to not be involved in the project suddenly wanted to be involved and go through the same transformation. The team that was part of the initial project adopted the new ways of working immediately and with enthusiasm. Suddenly, instead of only 20% of the workforce showing up in the office on any given day, 55-60% showed up. The teams used the different spaces to have ad hoc meetings, conduct presentations and have team briefings in the collaboration areas. They celebrated their successes together and shared personal days, such as birthdays, together. The sales performance increased by 8% and the satisfaction levels increased by 126%, at the time of measurement, which was 8 weeks after the change.

This was achieved by really understanding all the different influencing factors and people's needs not just from a business perspective but also from a personal perspective.

Key points

- Understand the internal and external influencing factors of the change to really assess readiness for change.
- The type of change determines the leadership style required for the change, not the other way round.
- Need to understand and utilise the "end person in mind" approach. Articulate the vision from the end person's perspective – what does it mean to them and hence why should they care about it?

Reflective questions

1. What are the external and internal influencing factors of the change?
2. Now you know what leadership style is required, how are you going to do it? Who are you going to do it to and how do you know you have been successful?
3. What does the person the furthest from the decision-making room think and feel about life, much less about the change?
4. Why should the end person in mind care about your change?

6

UNLEASH YOUR INNER POWER

Nothing great was ever accomplished without enthusiasm.
Ralph Waldo Emerson

You're stupid! You're ridiculous! That is impossible! Who do you think you are?

Many people think they don't have the strength or power or ability to achieve the things they want to achieve. They have been beaten down and told "no" or laughed at so many times that they have started to believe it themselves and hence don't feel they can make things happen. It is too difficult, impossible, ridiculous. The tools in this book will help you feel confident, powerful and empowered to achieve the goals you want to achieve; to feel you have the inner strength to make anything possible.

According to the British Medical Association (2024), the rates of mental illness have been steadily increasing in adults and at an even higher rate for children and young people over the past 5 years in the UK. Resilience is

DOI: 10.4324/9781003643692-6

often discussed as that aspect of mental health and coping which is paramount to the ability to spring back during adverse circumstances. However, being resilient helps people to manage stressful situations, protect them from mental ill-health and improve their health and wellbeing. At work, this ensures that people continue to do their job well and deliver at a high level.

When I was young, I became a professional dancer. However, that was quite a challenging road because in that environment I was criticised a great deal, and many times not in a nice way or about things I could change in any way, like my height. I was also told "no" a lot from professional schools where I wanted to study, as well as companies and shows I wanted to perform. Being constantly rejected in some way forces you to either build resilience or you end up crumbling. The way I handled each rejection was to figure out what it was I did "wrong" or what I could do better. At one of the first auditions I attended for a professional summer programme, I was taken into a room with 60 other girls, and within the first 10 minutes, I was cut by the audition panel. You may ask how could I learn anything from such a short experience, but what I discovered is this school were not interested in seeing my full ability through a class until they knew some immediate things about me – for example, how high my leg could go easily. So that was the first exercise they had us do and after that the first cut was made. As a result, I made sure the following year I was fully warmed up to get my leg as high as absolutely possible upon entering that room so I was not one of the first to be cut. And guess what – I made it through. I still never did get a place at that school, and I continued to try for three more years, but each time I went in to learn more about the audition panel and what they wanted, so I could do better the next time.

Many people find change stressful, challenging, difficult and daunting. For nearly three decades, across business we have talked about how change is continuous and yet we have not changed how we manage and lead change for ourselves, much less for others. Is it any wonder we then talk more about the resistance of change and burnout from change more than how we can actually help people in change?

So how do we build or rather re-build our resilience so we can cope mentally healthily during change in this unpredictable world?

Firstly, recognise we all have resilience within us already, and hence it is a skill, we need to nurture and build, not develop from scratch. Have you ever seen a baby cry for milk, a change of nappy or for sleep? And they won't stop crying until they get what they want – that is resilience.

We can build our resilience by writing down each day/week what went well for us, what not so well and hence what we should focus on next. Most of us tend to focus a great deal on what we feel did not go well or that we feel we messed up. But the reality many times is that more went well than not well. So, using this technique will help us focus on both elements – our achievements and our challenges. Then outlining what we need to focus on next enables us to put the learnings we just outlined in a way so we create a type of action plan on how we can do better next. After all, "There are no mistakes in life, only lessons," right?

We discussed earlier how we create a vision. To build our own personal resilience the vision can be either short, medium or long term, but we need to be very clear what it is we want to do/achieve/get to. If we can see what it is we are trying to achieve, then we have a much greater chance of actually achieving it. At the same time, if we are wishy washy with it, then how will we possibly know we have achieved anything because we have not defined it. Many have heard the analogy, "You can get there one step at a time." The question is to know what the step is so you can take it.

There is a children's book called *Little One Step* by Simon James (2003). It is about a little duckling and he found the journey home with his older brothers quite long and hard. So when he would stop and say he couldn't go on any more and wanted his mamma, his eldest brother challenged him to do "one step." He didn't know what that was, so his brother explained, "you just lift one foot up and say 1, then put it down and say 'step', and then you start again with the other foot." The little duckling then started saying "one step one step one step" with each step he took until they reached the clearing and found home.

Lastly we said before, change is not a one man band activity. It has been discussed and agreed multiple times across numerous journals/books/ platforms that people are the #1 critical factor for change – you cannot do change without people. You then may be saying "Yeah but it doesn't take more than one person to change a light bulb." The reality is though that it does take more than one person – A LOT MORE. We all don't make our own light bulbs. Quite a few other people did at a factory. Then several more pack-aged the lightbulb and yet other people then transported it from the factory to wholesaler and then to the retail outlets. Lastly other people were then involved in putting the lightbulb on the shelf for purchase. Now it may have been one person that then purchased the light bulb, went home and put it into the light fitting, but there were a lot of people involved in enabling that one person to "change" a light bulb.

We need to remember we always need help and support, even for the simplest of things. Building resilience, like building a structure, requires support. And that support is multifaceted. You will need cheerleaders to help spur you on, particularly at those really challenging moments. You need sponsors who make sure you have the right resources available to build like time, space, reflection, food, water, etc. They make sure you have what is needed to build the resilience. You also need a team to share the challenges and successes with, even if this is just through conversation of one other person. You need space to vent, celebrate, bounce ideas and explore thoughts.

As a result, a lot of people are involved with any type of change. Therefore, one of the most critical elements of leading and managing change is stakeholder management and engagement because you need to first understand who you are engaging, what is going on for them, what impact this will have on them and how do you need them engaged. What role do you need them to play, what do you need them to do and how and how often do you need them to do it, if anything? All this needs to be assessed, established and then a plan put in place for action.

Now this all may seem like Project Management 101, but the added element I would like to add here, and based on the Henley research shared earlier, this does not seem to be so obvious. The stakeholder plan needs to encompass all areas across the **whole** of the organisation – whether they are directly or indirectly impacted by the change. This is because you may need to elicit the help of HR or IT teams in an activity, even though they may not be directly impacted by the change itself. Knowing this is the case from the outset and assessing this, so that when you go to them you can clearly outline the parameters of their involvement and ask for help, is a much stronger position than not having this information and not being clear. Not everyone likes surprises, and most people do not seem to like surprises that they see as taking something away from them, whether that be time/headspace, etc.

A people-centric approach to stakeholder engagement goes beyond the transactional elements of change and instead focus on building meaningful connections that drives mutual value creation. To kick off the stakeholder plan, you need to list everyone who will be impacted either directly or indirectly and everyone whose help you may need to get it over the line. You then need to assess them in two ways:

1. Whether they are a potential champion, or a malvern (someone who is a great source of information or people) or a blocker.
2. Based on their level of influence and interest, whether you need them to champion the work and be actively involved on a regular basis, advocate the work and need to be kept informed, don't need much involvement but need to monitor to ensure they don't become a blocker or need their influence on other people or business areas and hence keep them satisfied with their engagement (Figure 6.1).

Using this approach to stakeholder engagement means you recognise the intrinsic value of individuals and emphasise the importance of understanding and addressing the needs, aspirations and concerns of people at all levels. Once you have completed this, you can then start to create your change impact assessment through initial conversations with your key stakeholders. This will give you an idea of the scale of the change, and by scale, I don't mean size in regard to numbers, but in significance of difference between the current state and future state in relation to the impact on people's hearts and minds, as well as workload.

It is well recognised that within any one organisation there is a culture, which is the invisible thread that weaves all the intricacies of an organisation together. These include the values, beliefs, norms and practices which underpin how decisions are taken and how people ultimately work within the organisation. However, sometimes that culture evolves slightly across different areas of the business, which can be tricky when you need to foster collaboration, innovation and changes in behaviours. These different internal cultures can arise through a variety of reasons:

1. Mergers and acquisitions – different identities coming together to create one.
2. Leadership changes – shift in priorities and sometimes values.
3. Generational differences – different expectations and preferences.
4. Functional differences – different modes of practice/type of work.
5. Organisational growth or sudden low performance – not having enough resources or too many.

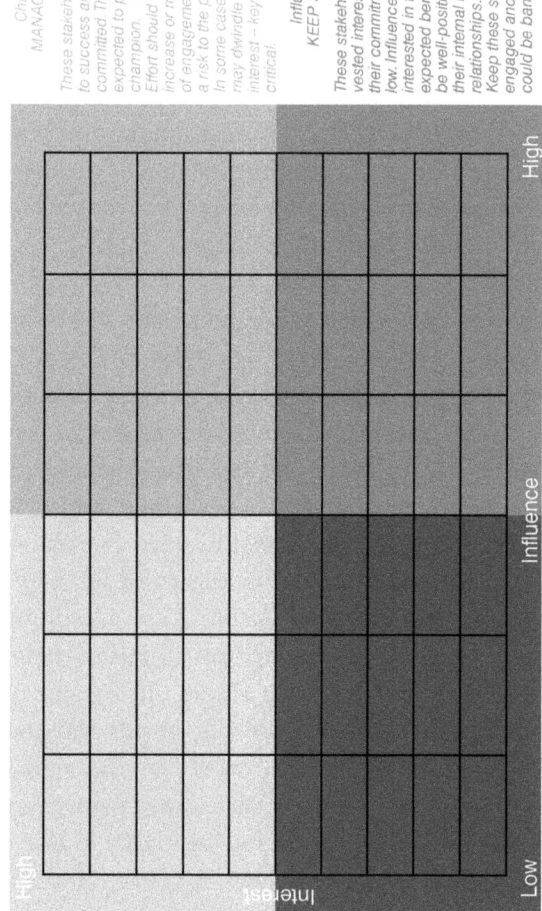

Champions
MANAGE CLOSELY

These stakeholders are Critical to success and they are highly committed. They can be expected to play the role of champion.
Effort should be made to increase or maintain their level of engagement or they could be a risk to the programme.
In some cases, over engagement may dwindle their level of interest – key messaging is critical.

Influencers
KEEP SATISFIED

These stakeholders have a vested interest in success but their commitment is medium-low. Influencers are most interested in the realisation of expected benefits and should be well-positioned to leverage their internal influence and relationships.
Keep these stakeholders fully engaged and satisfied or they could be barriers to success.

Advocates
KEEP INFORMED

These stakeholders are not Critical to success, but they are highly committed. They can be expected to play the role of advocate.
Keep these stakeholders adequately informed and continue to engage, to gauge any changing attitudes towards the programme.
Make use of their interest by using them as a support/ambassador.

Bystanders
MONITOR

These stakeholders are not very critical to success and their commitment is low. No action may be needed to change this group's commitment unless they become more critical to project success.
Regularly check and monitor these stakeholders to assess this. Aim to move these stakeholders to the right in terms of engagement.

High   Influence   Low

Interest   High

Figure 6.1 Stakeholder holder mapping matrix.

Any one of these reasons can create different internal cultures within one organisation, which is fine so long as they align with the broader organisational culture. However, if they diverge significantly, then large pockets of resistance can arise, there can be lower willingness to collaborate, which will decrease potential innovation and ultimately increase conflict across the organisation. This can lead to disengagement of staff, higher turnover rates than usual and inconsistent performance as people will not be feeling confident or secure. Leading and managing the change is not a "one size fits all" scenario – it will need to be managed differently in accordance with the different cultures and relationships within an organisation.

So, what is in a relationship? Relationships are something we have with everyone and everything – either as a concept or on a personal level or on a theoretical level or even on an emotional or moral level. Yet it is a word and concept that too easily is taken for granted; particularly in business: client relationship managers, client relationship systems, etc. It is as if we just actively manage a relationship, then all will be ok. However, relationships are more than that and require more than just us as a single entity to manage, as we discussed earlier.

First, it takes two to tango – two people need and want to be in the relationship in the first place. Desire, in other words, is required. Second, there needs to be trust and that takes some time to build. Third, it takes time because obtaining trust is not typically automatic – it takes time. Value is the fourth ingredient. People need to feel they get a value from the relationship, whether that value is love, feeling loved, obtaining knowledge, support, feeling good, being stimulated, encouraged, listened, etc.

These four different elements: desire, trust, time and value are all interconnected. You have to have the desire to want to give/receive the advice/guidance/help/love/ stimulation, etc., and you need the time to have the trust that what you are receiving is of actual value to you. Thus making relationships wonderful and challenging all at the same time. Throw in some emotion and you have your roller-coaster that we always feel like we are on, most of the time.

So, what is the point of all this?

It is to say we need to realise that the relationships we have, for whatever reasons and with whatever/whoever they may be, are our greatest asset because this is what makes each of us unique and enables us to be and do what and who we are.

Many times, when leaders and managers are trying to utilise the ABChange model, they state "the change is all these types, so how can I choose one?" Which is why, as discussed earlier, the type of change is dependent on the ultimate goal of the change – to improve, heal discourse, etc. However, with that said, there will be many other little changes underneath the overarching change, and this is predominantly due to the "clash of the internal cultures."

So how do we handle this? Well, at this point, it should come as no surprise to you that the first step is understanding where people are coming from in regard to their point of view of their place in the organisation and how they operate. Understanding the history from their perspective will give you a level of understanding that is many times ignored by leaders, thus enabling a level of empathy. You achieve this by having lots of open conversations and communications – recognise where people are coming from and the journey they will be embarking on with this change. There may need to be some adjustments to the internal cultures to help foster a level of unity with the vision of change, so this needs to be understood and recognised as well. Through the facilitation of focus groups, cross-functional workshops and training, the potential clash can be mitigated.

This requires strong change leadership and support from the wider change network. The leadership teams need to be aligned with the broader organisational vision for change and must role model the desired behaviours. If the change is for people to work in a hybrid way and work remotely 2 days a week, then the leaders need to work remotely 2 days a week. If the change is to not have single-use/person offices, and instead have quiet rooms or shared rooms, then the leader needs to not insist on having a personal office even for only the days they are in the office. The office will still be perceived as that particular leader's office, and the leader will be seen as not demonstrating the right behaviours, which creates exclusivity and impacts the overall level of adoption of the change as others will then believe they don't have to demonstrate the right behaviours either – only when it suits them. Now all this may sound obvious – but in reality it happens so often which means that the investment of change is not only greatly diminished, de-motivation and de-valuation of loyalty also diminishes.

In a financial services organisation, a team was implementing a new way of working that included hybrid working and unassigned seating for all. This was to enable a huge transition of the entire workforce into temporary accommodation whilst the old spaces were renovated. Now this transition was scheduled to last several years, as the construction of the new space was going to take a great deal of time to complete, which was widely understood and agreed. Unfortunately, there was a major lack of executive sponsorship and change leadership with this change, despite the fact that it was costing the organisation several billion pounds to implement and complete. As a result, when the transition to the temporary space began, a number of leaders felt they needed to be excluded from the new ways of working, including the CEO, and this meant the message of exclusivity cascaded throughout the organisation. Soon it became clear that due to this exclusivity, the amount of space acquired would not be enough and more was needed. This added to the cost of the change two-fold – delays in delivery and overhead costs in more space. This also cost the company a great deal of goodwill, collaboration and willingness to support the change as many then felt they were under-valued in comparison. In a world where talent competition is high, particularly in financial services, this is dangerous, as the company greatly risks losing their top talent to another financial services institution or even another financial services team to one that is seen as being more inclusive across the whole workplace.

The engagement activities are then built around reinforcing the desired vision. The ADKAR model is a useful method to use to build a series of activities that create a mix of different levels of engagement depending on where in the journey an individual is on the change (Creasey and Hiatt 2012). The model is built on five different steps an individual goes through when embarking on a change: awareness (aware it exists), desire (to make the decision to change), knowledge (of how to do it), ability (of actually doing it) and reinforcement (continuing to do it). Now, in some ways, these steps may seem obvious, and really they should; however, there are numerous times when a company starts a change project/programme and the first step has not even been thought through, much less communicated before they want to skip along to knowledge (i.e. the training) of the change, is incredible!

Furthermore, there needs to be a recognition that people will experience the change at different paces and in different ways. It is not possible to treat all the people impacted in the same way. There needs to be a variety of not only different activities for each of the different steps of the person's journey, but there needs to also be a variety of different channels and tactics used. For example, to develop an awareness of the change, a town hall (or several to accommodate different time zones) could be organised and recorded for future references. There can also be a follow-up of announcements on intranet pages, newsletters, team briefings, network briefings, awareness videos, podcasts, app alerts/notifications, not to mention the usual emails and internal chat platforms. Best practice is to use as many of these channels and tactics within an organisation for a host of reasons:

1. Not everyone is around or available on the "announcement" day.
2. Not everyone can attend the announcement at the time in which it is scheduled.
3. Everyone consumes information differently, and the most important goal here is that everyone has received the information. It is demotivating to find out people are not aware of the change for the person themselves, as they then feel "left out or excluded" in some way, as well as the project team.
4. As according to Creasey and Hiatt, it takes five to seven times before a piece of information is really remembered by a person. So even if an individual is at the announcement of the change, they may not remember all the information you need them to have, so it needs to be repeated several times, to ensure they definitely have all the information required.

Now you may think that five to seven times may sound like a lot, but, how many times have you told your child/partner/friend (fill in the blank) something and within less than a minute, they have forgotten it? For example, watching a child of 7–10 years old to "go brush your teeth/get your shoes on" and by the time the child got to the top of the stairs or the space to do these things and the task would be forgotten is laughable. However, if you were to say to that same child to do the task five to seven times in different creative ways on their way to the stairs, there is a much higher probability that the child would remember.

I have to admit, I did try this on my son when he was 7 and 8 years old because he invariably would "forget" to brush his teeth when I would go in to read and tuck him into bed. So, I started to say to him as he went up the stairs, "Now brush your teeth. Remember to brush your teeth. Teeth need to be brushed. You are going to brush your teeth, aren't you?" etc. When this happened the first few months, he found it funny, but he remembered.

Then he stopped finding it funny, but he still remembered, and after that it was a habit.

Remember back when we watched adverts, the ones that would repeat the company name or slogan multiple times in a 30-second ad? That is why they did it – because we would remember if we were told at least five to seven times; if we are only told once, the chances are, unfortunately, we won't remember. We many times have so much going on and can easily get distracted with an email, or sudden call, or chat from a colleague, that we can so easily forget something.

And all this is just for the first step on an individual's journey of change! There are four other steps that need to be implemented with equally the same or potentially more activities scheduled to help everyone along the process of change. The key element to remember is that throughout all these activities, the common vision will need to be repeated, reminded and reinforced throughout each and every activity. This can easily be done through branding – creating a logo/icon that illustrates the behavioural change. This can then be used in all the communications/engagements and activities, so people know what is going to be discussed before the talking/showing begins.

The next element though in creating people-centric, sustainable change is engagement. Unfortunately, we can create a whole host of different activities for all the different steps of the process, but just because we build it does not mean the people will come along. So, how do we get engagement for all these linked activities for the change?

The key step here is to have active and visible sponsorship and leadership for the change. In *Leading People in Change* (2021), the definitions of sponsorship and leadership and the differences between the two are defined in detail. To summarise, the sponsorship needs to be someone who has influence over the senior leadership team as it is the leadership team that will help lead people through the change. In both cases, there needs to be a real recognition and demonstration of the change. The key strategic messages need to be communicated first by the sponsor and reinforced by the leadership team. This illustrates to all individuals, not only the importance of the change, but also the fact that the change is critical for all to be aware of, make the decision to change, increase their knowledge so they can build their ability and help reinforce and embed the change. (See what I did there ☺: repeat five to seven times.)

I have worked on a number of projects when the executive sponsorship has been really strong through by being active and visible to all and when it has been really poor because of the exact opposite. The difference and impact of this executive sponsorship is huge and has the ability to make or break a change. When I was working with an infrastructure company on a digital programme, the executive sponsor made it very clear how this change was significant in the future of the organisation. They demonstrated this not just through their words but their actions – when we needed the senior leaders' support for activities, he would gladly send the email and reinforce the messages with his interactions with his team of what they needed to do and why, thus eliciting the support needed for the change. At every opportunity, he would galvanise enthusiasm for the change and share his vision on how this was going to make a huge difference to what they did and how they did it in amazingly positive ways. As the senior change manager of this programme, it was super inspiring to witness. Another time, I was working with a technology company and the executive sponsor was so keen to see the change happen, if there was a senior leader that would try to cast doubt on the opportunity, he would quickly pull them aside and share with them the negative impact this could have on the overarching change and hence why it was important that they showed support to help the teams achieve better results – bringing people down was only going to have negative consequences and this was not something the teams could afford. This positive leadership and executive sponsorship was contagious, as a result, and really generated an uplifting feeling across the whole division.

However, in a different organisation, I was part of a larger change team on a digital programme and unfortunately the actual executive sponsor was uninvolved and inactive with the change. They were present as a figurehead of the organisation and talked about the digital change, but they were not a part of it, so if something was needed to help galvanise support, they were not present, and instead the role would fall to the change leadership. Now you may think so long as it was done then all is fine. But the reality is that because the leadership had to go to their peers in the organisation to affectively "as for a favour" to obtain support, the support was patchy. This resulted in higher levels of resistance and stronger stakeholder management at lower levels because there wasn't the active and visible support and sponsorship from the top making the change a priority for the whole organisation.

Key points

- Resilience is something we are all born with – what we need to do is nurture what we already have by feeding it so our resilience gets bigger and bigger.
- Within every organisation and workplace, there are multiple sub-cultures.
- The same change will need to be approached and lead slightly differently depending on the sub-cultures.
- Widen the stakeholder mapping, analysis and engagement so the whole organisation is assessed, not just the immediate "programme/project" individuals.

Reflective questions

1. Who do you need to include in your stakeholder map and analysis and have you covered all the business areas?
2. What support will your stakeholders need and what do you need from them?
3. What are the sub-cultures within your workplace?
4. What will you need to do differently as a result of these sub-cultures?

7

A COMMUNITY OF CHANGE

An absence of controversy never affirms good performance....

Alison Taylor

Many organisations and people talk about the need for a change network, but few know what to or how to create/build one, much less maintain one. How many organisations have you experienced that go through a great deal of investment to create and build and change network just for it to die within a few months of the announcement?

A change network is a community of people within an organisation, so the elements involved in creating, building and maintaining it should not be under-estimated, especially considering this is typically an additional responsibility to the "day job." At the same time, the value a change network brings to an organisation and people must also not be undervalued. We have discussed several times how we as leaders and managers of change cannot be "gurus of all information" and how change is not a "one man band activity." A change network is a critical tool in delivering change

DOI: 10.4324/9781003643692-7

and without it there is NO WAY anyone can deliver a people-centric change or a sustainable change successfully.

Establishing a well-designed change network that includes champions offers numerous benefits that can significantly enhance an organisation's ability to navigate transformation effectively:

1. **Improved communication and engagement**
   One of the most critical components of any change initiative is communication. Traditional top-down communication models often fail to resonate with employees at all levels. A change network, however, allows for more two-way communication. Change champions, being embedded within teams, can translate high-level messages into contextually relevant information that resonates with their peers. They can also collect feedback and share insights back up the chain, ensuring that leadership remains attuned to employee concerns and morale.

   By involving employees directly in the change process, organisations can increase engagement and reduce resistance. People are more likely to support changes when they understand the rationale behind them and see colleagues they trust endorsing the initiative.

2. **Faster adoption of change**
   Change networks accelerate adoption by reducing the time it takes for new behaviours, tools, or processes to become normalised. Change champions serve as early adopters who model desired behaviours and offer peer-to-peer support, which often carries more weight than top-down mandates. This grassroots influence helps shift group norms and reduces the learning curve for others.

   For example, when rolling out a new technology platform, change champions can provide hands-on assistance, offer informal training and share tips in a way that feels accessible and less intimidating than formal training alone. This speeds up the integration of new systems into everyday work.

3. **Enhanced localised implementation**
   Change rarely affects all parts of an organisation in the same way. A centralised approach can overlook the unique challenges and nuances of different departments or regions. Change networks ensure that local insights are taken into account and that solutions are tailored to

specific contexts. Change champions act as translators and customisers, adjusting implementation plans to fit the culture, workflows and needs of their local environments.

This localisation not only improves effectiveness but also shows respect for the diversity within an organisation, increasing overall buy-in.

4. **Stronger cultural alignment**

   Culture plays a critical role in the success of any change effort. Change networks help embed new values and norms across the organisation by creating a coalition of role models. When people see their leaders and peers embracing and advocating for a change, it signals a cultural shift in a more tangible and relatable way than leadership speeches or posters ever could.

   Over time, change networks help to reinforce and sustain new behaviours, making them part of the cultural fabric. This is especially useful in long-term transformations such as digital adoption, diversity and inclusion initiatives or agile ways of working.

5. **Increased trust and credibility**

   Employees are more likely to trust information and guidance when it comes from someone they know and respect. Change champions typically hold influence within their teams, not necessarily because of their title, but because of their relationships and reputations. Their credibility adds legitimacy to the change initiative and makes people feel more confident in the direction the organisation is heading.

   Moreover, involving employees in shaping and implementing change builds a sense of ownership. It signals that leadership values their input and recognises their expertise, further strengthening organisational trust.

6. **Early identification of risks and barriers**

   A change network serves as an early warning system. Because change champions are embedded in the day-to-day operations of various parts of the organisation, they are well positioned to spot resistance, confusion or breakdowns before they escalate into major issues. This allows leaders to proactively address concerns, adapt strategies and offer targeted support where it's needed most.

   Without a change network, these issues may remain hidden until it's too late to course-correct.

7. **Capacity building and leadership development**
    Establishing a change network is also an opportunity to develop future leaders. Change agents gain experience in strategic thinking, communication, influence and problem-solving skills that are essential for leadership roles. Organisations that invest in building and supporting these networks often find they are also cultivating a pipeline of talent ready to take on larger responsibilities.

Creating a change network

Creating a change network needs to be included in the readiness activities of any change. This requires an establishment and hence agreement of the different roles in the network, what activities are involved for each role, time commitment and expectations (Table 7.1).

Beyond the different role allocations outlined above, you need the change network to ultimately support colleagues throughout the transition. Now the specifics of what this will look like will depend on the organisation itself and the actual change you are implementing, but in general you need the network to encourage adoption with a positive outlook. This does not mean you need everyone going around with a happy smile on their face and saying everything is wonderful, when it clearly is not. It does mean you need people to be objective though, not destructive – and there is a huge difference. If someone is being deliberately destructive, then it most likely is time to have that difficult conversation with them about whether the new direction is the right direction for them, and ultimately the organisation. This may sound harsh, but a recognition that a new direction is going to be the right direction for everyone is required – in other words, with a dose of realism, the new direction may be the right one for the organisation as a whole, but not everyone in the organisation.

The change network will also need to make sure that regular team briefings include updates on the change itself and model the new ways of working. There is nothing more destructive of a change than a leader, particularly a senior leader, talking to their teams about the change and what needs to happen, just for themselves to actually not demonstrate the behaviours. Those actions illustrate an "it's ok for you but not me – I am an exception." This ultimately undermines any and all change.

Table 7.1 Roles and Expectations in a Change Network

Role	Expectation
Executive Sponsor	Actively and visibly sponsors the change by sending out key strategic messages and participating in change activities and events.
Change Leader	Actively and visibly leads the change by cascading key strategic and operational messages and participating in change activities and events. Ensures all the right resources are readily available to support the change.
Change Manager	Lynchpin for all change communications and activities. Actively and visibly builds and maintains the change network and collaborates with the change team to ensure all parties are fully aware of change requirements. Applies the process, structures and tools of empowering others through the change journey.
Change Champion	Active and visible "on the ground" conduit between the project team/change manager and staff. Typically, they are the team influencers who others look to for information and knowledge within an organisation. Should not typically be managers, as there is a large time commitment, or administrators as they need to be key team influencers. Create local change activities to help build the "desire," enthusiasm and excitement for the change. Seen as the "go-to" local person for Q&A from staff.
Line Managers	Support direct reports through the change by allowing resources to be available as and when required. Encourages team members to attend change activities and events.
Staff/Employees	Explore, embrace, adopt and use the change.

Furthermore, the change network will need to help people know what and how the change is going to work and happen, so they need to be able to address any questions and concerns, point people in the direction of knowledge/learning and recognise and mitigate resistance. Oh yes, our favourite word has finally raised itself with change – RESISTANCE. In *Leading in Change: A Practical Guide* (2021), I outline all the different ways someone can resist and how to mitigate them, so I am not going to reiterate the tactics here. I am going to reinforce the message though that resistance will happen, and it is ok – it is natural and human to resist, so we all will have to deal with it. The key to resistance is knowing what it may look like, sound like and be, so we can use key tactics to mitigate it. This is one of the key benefits of change not being a one man band activity because there is a network of people to help.

Lastly the change network needs to recognise success, and this needs to be across the whole organisation. Celebrating success, whether that is recognising an individual who has demonstrated the change well, or a team or the whole organisation, is critical. It recognises the challenges faced and conquered and reinforces the direction and why it is important. Recognition does not always need to be big or expensive, but it does need to be done and it needs to be felt as a genuine appreciation.

So how do you go about identifying the right people for the different roles in the network? First, it is to look at the organisational structure and identify people who may already be in a position of influence. It is also to understand the different groups across the organisation that may have influence and what could be considered a good deal of "soft power" for one reason or another. Once you understand the different influencing groups and individuals, you can start to piece together the change network.

Identifying the executive sponsor

Identifying the executive sponsor vs the change leadership can be the trickiest task, simply because it is typically wrapped up in the politics of an organisation. The person who is responsible for instigating the change can many times be confused as the executive sponsor, but in reality they are the change leader. This is due to the fact that the executive sponsor needs to be the person at the top that can influence and galvanise motivation to act, when needed. For example, in technology change, many times the CIO is considered the executive sponsor, but the reality is they are the change leader and the executive sponsor needs to be the CEO because it is the CEO that can then influence and motivate the HR Director to act; whereas if the CIO goes to the HR Director, they are peers and it ends up being seen and delivered as a favour, not a priority of the organisation.

The main characteristics of an executive sponsor are to be active and visible, happy to engage with colleagues outside scheduled events, role model the change, communicate directly and are committed and aware of the impact on the business. To help them, it is necessary to update them on a regular basis.

Identifying the change leadership

Typically, the change leadership is at several different levels within an organisation. You can have the leader who is responsible for the delivery of the change, for example the CIO in the above situation. You can also have a group of change leaders that are identified as being the "future leaders of the organisation," and this is many times the level below the executive level or can even be that senior/middle leadership level. They can also be engagement groups that have been identified to help promote certain organisational priorities such as sustainability, inclusion, etc. Whatever the case may be, their main role is to be the influencers of change and to ensure the right resources are in place to deliver.

The main characteristics of a change leader are to be an authority of change, to build a coalition of support, identify and involve resources required for delivery and actively and visibly be involved. There is nothing worse than someone having the position of a change leader and not being actively and visibly involved – in fact, this can be quite detrimental to the delivery of the change. So ensuring they have the tools and resources to act along with the authority and motivation is critical.

Identifying a champion

A change champion network is needed for the simple reason that it is impossible to manage/influence the behaviours of thousands of people by yourself, as the change/project manager or even as a project team. Remember, earlier we discussed how change is not a "one man band activity." This is one of the main reasons why! Prosci have done some research into how people receive communications and what they do with them. In their research, they state that if a CEO sends out an email, 47% of people are likely to open it and if a change/IT/HR/project manager sends an email, 2–3% of people are likely to open it (2020). We have no idea if that percentage has read the email, but there is still a high degree of people who have not bothered to even open the email! However, if a team member or line manager sends out an email, 69% of people are likely to open it. This is because when we work with someone on a daily basis, we feel more obliged and curious to find out what they are communicating to us. Therefore, to increase the probability that the key messages and information are communicated to individuals on the change, the best method is to have a change champion, whose role is to ensure the messages are given to all their representatives and they are able to go through the ADKAR people process of change.

So the champion needs to not typically be a senior manager because they many times do not have the time to commit to the activities of a champion. The champion also needs to not typically be the team administrator because they do not necessarily have the influence the champion needs across the team. So what type of person do you need to be a change champion?

Firstly you need to recognise that you typically need 1 champion per 100 people plus a deputy. A deputy is included because the duties cannot all fall onto one person, as that creates a single point of failure. Not to mention the fact that not everyone can be in the office at all times – we are generally working in a hybrid world and there are holidays and sick days, personal days, etc. So you need to have a second person to help and make sure that the whole team is aware and know what and how to do things at any given time.

Secondly you need to recognise that a champion will also typically need at least 7 hours per month, outside of their day job to spend on the change activities itself. If you think about it, if they are responsible for 100 people, let's say there are 4 smaller teams within that 100 people that all have weekly or fortnightly team meetings. If the main activity that champion does is attend the team meetings to cascade information, that already equates to 4 hours at least, and then there is the monthly group champion meeting and then that only leaves 2 hours a month to spend on sending and replying to emails, etc. So, in reality, 7 hours a month is not very much and yet it is outside of the day job, which will also be busy. So, leaders and managers need to make sure that they nominate someone who will genuinely be able to have the time. Many times, this person is seen as the social butterfly, but not always. The person does need to be someone others trust though to not only tell them the truth but to tell others the truth and hence feel represented – people need to feel any feedback or questions they have on the change will be communicated by their change champion to whoever is necessary and hence answers are returned. Thus creating a 360-degree feedback loop on the change, which allows people to feel a part of it and hence on the journey, rather than feel like it is being done to them.

Thirdly, it is important you don't want just a "yes" person as a champion – you want someone who will question and challenge, so they are keeping in mind the genuine perspectives of the people they represent at the fore. However, you also do not want a "negative nelly" – someone who is just going to be negative all the time for the sake of it. You want someone who will be objective but also be up for helping others.

The champion needs to be active and visible throughout the change/transition, who can easily build or already has a coalition of peers and colleagues, who communicates directly with team members clearly and regularly, able to attend townhall meetings, roadshows, etc, is happy to walk the floor and engage with colleagues in person and virtually outside of scheduled events, someone who can role model the desired behaviours and "walk the walk." Ultimately, you need someone who can build awareness, create the desire for others to change, provide the knowledge and reinforce the change.

Now that may all sound like a tall order, and it is, so you need to make sure you not only nominate wisely, but also that the person is up for the job as well. You should not just nominate and wait for the change team to then contact them with the new role being a surprise to the individual. You be saying to yourself, "well of course not" but you would be surprised how many times this happens. Remember we are embarking on a people-centric change, and your role as a change leader and/or line manager, as described early, is to support the change and that means talking to your people about it.

The key responsibilities of a change champion are to be a keen learner, coach, liaise, advocate and role model, so ask your teams if there is someone who is keen to build their coaching skills or who loves to learn new things – they may be the perfect person for the job of a change champion.

When it comes to identifying champions, you need to plan more time than you ever think possible. Why? Because you are relying on people to identify someone within a certain timescale and let's face it, they have their day job to do and so with this being out of that scope, it will take people time. When I was working with a local government organisation, I set aside 6 weeks, thinking really it should take no more than 4, so I will plan an extra 2 weeks for good measure. Well, even I had not anticipated the need for more time. In the end, we ended up sending out several reminder emails and in some instances phoned people asking them for their nominations. In the end, we got there but it took a total of 8 weeks just to get them identified and confirmed.

However, it never ceases to amaze me the enthusiasm and energy in a room where you are kicking off the champion network. Does that mean there aren't cynics in the room – of course not. But even the cynics can't help but get a little giddy on the prospect of being at the forefront of change and having the opportunity to learn about things before their colleagues. The key benefits of a person being a champion are:

1. **Career growth**
   - Raises your profile within the organisation.
   - Increases your internal network across all areas of the business, which also increases your understanding of different business areas/institutions.
   - Develop leadership skills.
2. **Job satisfaction**
   - Get to know information first.
   - Feel a sense of purpose by contributing to major change.
   - Be empowered by being able to advocate ideas and bring about improvements.
   - Help shape solutions.
3. **Personal development**
   - Obtain continuous learning by being exposed to new technologies and methodologies regularly.
   - Build influencing and communication skills.
   - Build resilience by having to manage resistance to change and how to deal with setbacks whilst keeping moving forward.

However, with this great opportunity comes great responsibility. This is why it is important to promote the champions across the organisation. Simply, the promotion informs people who is their representative that they can go to for questions and ideas, but it also raises the profile of the champion. People start to recognise them and see them beyond the team influencer they have been and start to see them as an organisational influencer. This means that not only their colleagues know them and seek them out for information, but people who they don't typically work with in other teams also recognise them, including leaders across the organisation. This, for some, can seem daunting, but it can also be quite exciting and help in building that personal brand and professional career.

This is why I become a bit of a mother hen to the champions – they can be and feel quite exposed and some people sometimes take advantage of the champion network and think because they exist as a group they can be used for anything at any time. A couple of times, when I was launching the promotion and the kick-off event was still a month away, which is typical, leaders started to think they could immediately use the network for the change. But the reality is that before the kick-off session happens, the champions don't entirely know what the role entails in detail, much less what the change is about and what they can do to help. So, to ask them to get involved before the kick off, is not viable. I mean, how can you ask somebody to do something, when they don't even know what it is they are doing or what it is for and about? Insane really!

Having a change network in place and people actively and visibly in these roles is absolutely critical for any organisational change. It bridges the gap between strategy and execution, accelerates adoption, builds cultural alignment and empowers employees to become active participants in shaping their organisation's future. The benefits – ranging from improved communication and trust to faster implementation and reduced risk – far outweigh the effort required to build and maintain such a network. Organisations that embrace this approach will not only navigate change more effectively but also build a more resilient and agile workforce for the long term.

I shared earlier that change is not a one man band activity – it is also not a one team activity. It takes everyone to come on board and embark on the journey together. Typically, a change team is quite small and an organisation is much bigger, so to be able to influence across the whole organisation, there needs to be people at different levels talking, engaging, motivating, inspiring, laughing, questioning, challenging, testing, exploring all the different elements of change in order for it to be successful.

I was working in a public sector organisation, and there was an individual who had been with the organisation for quite some time. They were seen as the team influencer, but the reality for them was quite different. They were looking for something more in their role in the organisation. They had anticipated to receive a promotion, but due to some financial cut-backs, this did not happen, and they were feeling quite demotivated to say the least. The organisation was about to embark on a technology change – a new ERP programme, when a request for change champions went out to all the leaders across the business. Their line manager decided to nominate them for the role, and after talking to the individual, it was agreed they would become a champion. When I initially met this person, they were a bit sceptical as to whether the role was really what "was advertised," but when I assured them it was, which was why I was contacting them, because I needed a picture they were happy for us to use so we could promote them across the business, their attitude changed completely. They started to become brighter, they smiled and clearly showed a sense of pride in being asked to do the role. At the kick-off event, they met all the other champions across the organisation, received some swag that would help others identify them as champions and got training on how to be a champion. At the end of the event, when everyone else was leaving, they came up to me and said they were so happy to be asked to be a champion and they wanted to thank me for making them feel valued again. I told them it was not me, it was their line manager, which made them beam even more. It was only my responsibility now to make sure they got all the help they needed to do the role, so if they needed anything, they could reach out to me personally. This person could not have been more happy or have a bigger smile on their face if they tried – it was beautiful to see.

Key points

- A change network involves several layers within an organisation, all with different responsibilities, but ultimately accountable for the success of the change.
- A change champion is a team influencer within teams – not middle management because they don't have the time, and not necessarily the administrator because they don't always have the influence.
- Leaders must role model the required new behaviours; otherwise, exclusivity will generate resentment.

Reflective questions

1. Have you defined the commitment and requirements for each of the roles in the change network?
2. Have you identified the right people and obtained their approval along with their line manager's approval to ensure fully commitment?
3. Do you have champions identified in teams that are indirectly impacted as well as directly impacted?
4. Have you got all the right materials in place and resourced so everyone knows who they are and how to contact them?

CONCLUSION

The world is increasingly subject to significant change, and whilst the focus is often on the potential implications of exponential technology developments like artificial intelligence, robotics, adaptive manufacturing, augmented and virtual reality, for example, political, economic and social change are also happening at breakneck speed. This range of future forces—together with the current pandemic—act on life, society and business and add to our personal and organisational sense of complexity and uncertainty.

In the past, we have been confident in our predictions about how the external environment is evolving and been able to come to a consensus about the way ahead. Increasingly we are far from certain about how the outside world is evolving and are less able to reach consensus about how to proceed. It's this situation that we believe calls for a new focus to leading change in organisations, and that's not easy. There's a temptation to always do what we've always done. But then we get what we've always got; except the reality is that the world moves on and we risk being left behind.

DOI: 10.4324/9781003643692-8

Change management is about people and this statement of the obvious too often gets lost in over-complicated methodologies and technology-focused approaches to change.

There are a number of books out there on leadership and on change and on leading change. However, despite all this, many of us are still not getting it right and this is costing organisations a great deal of money and a great deal in people, from a loss of talent to lawsuits to recruitment fees.

There is a great deal of discussion on a variety of different workplace strategies in regard to hybrid working, technology and generative AI, UN sustainability goals and the societal shifts and realignments. All of this is compounding into what can feel like, to any leader, a big ball of mess. It may be difficult to see what the possible solutions could be, much less how to even start to go about doing them.

With the current environment especially, a number of questions arise concerning the nature of change and the human face of change. There needs to be a new mindset to accept and embrace exponential change, to do so with more than an eye on plausible multiple technology-centric futures, and enable a more human-centric future. This requires more of a renaissance leadership stance – need to start to ask more questions, rather than feel the need to answer them. The key question, "how else could this be done" and obtaining different answers from a whole host of different perspectives is paramount.

Are we building a change programme that takes us towards a single, perhaps preferred future, or to help us prepare for a number of potentially different futures? Building flexibility, agility and resilience into change programmes by exploring plausible scenarios is crucial for the future growth of our enterprises and the well-being of employees.

Using the holistic approach in the context of these different future scenarios enables leaders to generate a pathway that includes the people and ensures they are taken along this journey of change. This ensures an organisation's "greatest asset" is paid proper attention to whether changes are seen as radical or incremental. It marries the person and the change task together in the different future scenarios.

Many leaders find leading people through change intimidating because there are emotions involved, sometimes difficult conversations, and it takes people out of their comfort zones. With the current environment, we have all been very much outside our comfort zones for a whole variety of reasons.

However, if an organisation has answered the difficult question as to "what do they want to be" and done so from a people perspective, then so many of these challenges and questions that seem difficult to answer become easier. This is simply because if we know what we want to be, then we can ask ourselves does x take us closer to achieving what we want to be or further away.

Furthermore, why the vision is the right vision for the organisation also needs to be defined, and this needs to be well beyond the management spiel of "efficiencies and effectiveness." Whenever an organisation is changing and/or adopting a different operating model, people need to understand what difference this is going to make to their lives, what is needed for them to do things differently and why they should care and hence make the change in the first place.

Organisations can also struggle with the impact of a change on their people, processes and procedures due to the fast rate and/or amount of change they are dealing with. As a result, the culture of the organisation needs to be taken into consideration, as this can determine how ready the organisation is for the change. Furthermore, if the culture is not considered, then the change can be completely undermined and as a result, fail.

So, to be clear, you are NOT a change leader for the future if:

- You only consider the project team in your stakeholder engagement.
- Your vision is nebulous and unclear.
- You view the change from a very narrow perspective.

Analysing the external and internal influencing factors will help determine the type of change which defines the approach and activities within any change plan. However, we need to remember to take into consideration any assumptions that have been made along the way to ensure the plans are fit for all involved. Using the ABChange model will ensure the right leadership style and change skills are used at the appropriate time and place that fits within the specific contexts of the organisational change.

One of the keys to a culture change is stakeholder engagement and management. It is not enough to simply communicate (or what I call download information) to the key stakeholders. This is about taking them on the journey – enabling them to be a champion, critical friend, sponsor of the change. The key difference is to share what needs to be achieved and why but also how and get their input, so it can be put into action

In order to integrate real transformation, you need to embed the change into how an organisation does things – in the processes, procedures and the way it interacts. When it comes to workplace change, typically the process and procedures are thoroughly considered but rarely is the "interaction" of an organisation. The interaction involves the behaviours, communication mechanisms and socialisation which are part of the everyday working life of the organisation.

So, when implementing workplace change, you need to consider not just how you want people to interact in the future, but identifying and tackling the ways in which that is different from the way things take place today. Then you need to work with the people that are affected and ask them, "what do you need to do differently and how" or rather "what and how could you do things differently?" This is a very powerful way of not only giving owner-ship of the change to the people affected but also of implementing culture change. After all, it is the people that change a culture – whether that is in an organisation, city or society...not what's written on a piece of paper.

There have been a lot of catch phrases used in this book to help articu-late and embed people-centric change:

- Change is about people not rocket science, meaning leading change is about leading people.
- Change is not a one man band activity.
- None of us have a crystal ball.
- Need to know what people are thinking and feeling.

All of these catch phrases are driving a new mindset, a new way of leading change, that embodies a people-focused approach. In this book, we have discussed the elephant in the room, the biggest disruptors of our time, creating psychological safety in leading change, how to create sustainable change and build a vision from a people perspective, how to use and apply the holistic approach and how to unleash your inner power, so you have resilience as a leader of change.

To achieve all of this using the holistic approach, a variety of tools have been shared:

- Foresight.
- Organisational development.

- Visioning.
- ABChange model.
- Stakeholder mapping and engagement.
- Change network.

The ultimate aim of this book is to give you a practical method of approaching your change that will enable you to lead your people in change because that is what change is all about in the end – people.

A peer shared the story of the "Wizard of Oz" (Baum 1900) in a different perspective that is relevant to the key lessons in this book.

- Dorothy is lost and needs to find her way back home...follow the yellow brick road (YOUR VISION).
- She meets a scarecrow who needs a brain...(KNOWLEDGE – BE OPEN TO LEARN AND UNLEARN).
- She meets a tin man who needs a heart...(EMOTIONS – WILL BE INVOLVED).
- She meets a lion who needs courage...(BE BRAVE – TAKE SOME CHANCES AND ASK QUESTIONS).
- The Wizard can make all their wishes come true...
- If only...
- But he does tell her this very IMPORTANT truth...
- "She has all the power she needs to get home - it lies within her. It always has."

As a leader, it is our duty to always be learning – discovering, questioning, challenging, testing, listening. These skills and tasks are what help us shape the present and build a thriving future.

If there is one thing you take away from this book, I would encourage you to be a people explorer. Explore the emotions going on, how they are being expressed, not expressed, what are they doing, not doing, saying, not saying. Be a people explorer. That is the best and most successful way of leading change.

REFERENCES

Aguilar, F. (1967). *Scanning the Business Environment*. Macmillan: New York.

Baum, F. (1900). *The Wizard of Oz*. George M. Hill, Company: Chicago.

British Medical Journal (2024). *Mental Health Pressures in England*. https://www.bma.org.uk/advice-and-support/nhs-delivery-and-workforce/pressures/mental-health-pressures-data-analysis#:~:text=Demand%20for%20mental%20health%20services%20is%20rising&text=For%20children%20and%20young%20people,more%20than%201%20in%206

Brown, B. (2020). Braving Trust: The Seven Elements of Trust in LinkedIn. https://www.linkedin.com/pulse/braving-trust-bren%C3%A9-brown/

Bryan, J. (2021). *Leading People in Change: A Practical Guide*. Hero Press: London.

Bryan, J. (2022). Building Workplace Resilience in a Changing Environment, *Workplace Insight Magazine*. https://workplaceinsight.net/building-resilience-in-a-changing-environment/

Bryan, J. (2024a). A New Renaissance in Leading Change at the Most Disruptive Time in History, *Workplace Insight Magazine*. https://workplaceinsight.net/a-new-renaissance-in-leading-change-at-the-most-disruptive-time-in-history/

Bryan, J. (2024b). A Lightbulb Moment About Mental Health and Managing Change, *Workplace Insight Magazine*. https://workplaceinsight.net/a-lightbulb-moment-about-mental-health-and-managing-change/

Bryan, J. and Higgins, J. (2022). Hybrid Working and How We Escape the Constraints of Leadership, *Workplace Insight Magazine*. https://workplaceinsight.net/hybrid-working-and-escaping-the-constraints-of-leadership/

Bryan, J. and Higgins, J. (2023). *Leading Change in an Unpredictable World in Managing Change During Unprecedented Times*. IGI Publications: New York.

Bryan, J. Varney, S. and Wells, S. (2023). Adopting Foresight in People-Centric Change in *Henley Business School of Management Research Forum Report* 15 March 2023.

Callahan, C. The Biggest Generative AI Blunders of 2023, *Worklife.* December 18, 2023. https://www.worklife.news/technology/generative-ai-blunders-2023/#:~:text= In%20November%2C%20Sports%20Illustrated%20made,sites%20selling%20AI% 2Dgenerated%20headshots

Ciccomascolo, G. (2024). Microsoft vs Apple: Who Will Win the Market Cap Race? In CCN website https://www.ccn.com/analysis/microsoft-apple-market-cap-race/

Cowan, J. (2021). *Poor software quality cost the US$2.08trn in 2020* in The Evolving Enterprise. https://www.theee.ai/2021/01/06/6838-poor-software-quality-cost-the-usd-2-08- tn-in-2020/

Creasey, T. and Hiatt, J. (2012). *Change Management: The People Side of Change.* Prosci: Fort Collins.

Cunha, D., Inman, R.A., Faria, V., Moreira, P.A.S. and Rocha, M. (2020). Applying the Transtheoretical Model to Adolescent Academic Performance Using a Person-Centred Approach: A Latent Cluster Analysis in *Learning and Individual Differences.* Vol. 78. https://www.sciencedirect.com/science/article/abs/pii/S1041608019301542# preview-section-references

Daniel, W. (2024). 2023 was a Worse Year for Corporate Bankruptcies than 2020—and the Highest Since the GFC—After a Stunning 72% Surge, S&P Global Finds, *Fortune Online Magazine.* https://fortune.com/2024/01/09/how-many-businesses-bankrupt-covid-pandemic-2020-2023-global-financial-crisis/

de Bono, E. (2009). *Think! Before It's Too Late.* Vermilion: London.

Fenton-Jarvis, S. (2022). *The Human Centric Workplace.* LID Publishing: London.

Gartner (2024). Human Leadership: How HR Can Develop Your Organization's Leaders. https://www.gartner.com/en/human-resources/insights/human-leadership

Garton, E. Mankins, M. and Schwartz, D. (2021). Future Proofing Your Organisation, *Harvard Business Review.* https://hbr.org/2021/09/future-proofing-your-organization

Gates, William H. (1 January 1995). Horizon Scanning: Opportunities Technology Will Bring by 2005. *Journal of Business Strategy,* 16(1), 19–21. https://doi.org/10.1108/ eb039676

Green, V. (1992). *Good Mourning: What Death Teaches Us about Life.* Mirrors Publishing: New York.

Horrell J., Lloyd, H., Sugavanam, T., Close, J., and Byng, R. (2018). Creating and Facilitating Change for Person-Centred Coordinated Care (P3C): The Development of the Organisational Change Tool, *Health Expectations.* Wiley on line: https:// onlinelibrary.wiley.com/doi/full/10.1111/hex.12631#hex12631-bib-0011

Hunter-Torricke, D. (2024). *CIPD Festival of Work Conference.*

Igbinoba, B. (2023). The Cost of Project Failure — People, Processes and Technology, *Medium Online Magazine.* https://medium.com/agileinsider/the-cost-of-project-failure-people-processes-and-technology-5acbd4806721

James, S. (2003). *Little One Step.* Walker Books Ltd: London.

Kingsmen Software Blog (2 November 2021). The True Cost of a Failed Project. https:// www.kingsmensoftware.com/blog/cost-of-a-failed-project

Kotter, J. (1996). *Leading Change.* Harvard Business School Press: Boston. http://www. hbsp.harvard.edu

Lewin, K. (1935). *A Dynamic Theory of Personality.* New York: McGraw-Hill.

Lloyd, H., et al. (2017). *How to Use Metrics, Measures & Insights to Commission Person Centred Coordinated Care.* NHSE; http://p3c.org.uk/P3C_CommissionersGuide.pdf

McKinsey Report: COVID-19: Implications for Business and Executive Briefing. April 13 2022. https://www.mckinsey.com/capabilities/risk-and-resilience/our-insights/covid-19-implications-for-business

Mitchell, P. (2019). *A Dangerous Woman*. Hachette Book Group: New York.

Moreira, P., Faria V., Cunha, D., Inman, R. and Rocha, M. (2020). Applying the Transtheoretical Model to Adolescent Academic Performance Using a Person-centered Approach: A Latent Cluster Analysis, *Learning and Individual Differences, 78* https://www.sciencedirect.com/science/article/abs/pii/S1041608019301542#preview-section-references

Nauck, F., Pancaldi, L., Poppensieker, T. and White, O. (17 May 2021). The Resilience Imperative: Succeeding in Uncertain Times, *McKinsey and Company Report*. https://www.mckinsey.com/business-functions/risk-and-resilience/our-insights/the-resilience-imperative-succeeding-in-uncertain-times

Oxford Dictionary (2023). https://www.oxfordlearnersdictionaries.com/definition/english/trust_2#:~:text=trust%20to%20believe%20that%20somebody,me%20not%20to%20tell%20anyone

Prochaska, J. O., & DiClemente, C. C. (1982). Transtheoretical Therapy: Toward a more Integrative Model of Change. *Psychotherapy: Theory, Research & Practice, 19*(3), 276–288. https://doi.org/10.1037/h0088437

Prosci. (2016). https://www.prosci.com/

Richter, F. (2024). Microsoft Pulls Ahead (Again) in Long Rivalry With Apple, *Statista*. https://www.statista.com/chart/16255/market-capitalization-apple-microsoft/

Rinne, A. (2021). *Flux: 8 Superpowers for Thriving in Constant Change*. Berrett-Koehler Publishers: Oakland.

Russell, D. (2018). Mott MacDonald.

Senge, P. (1990). *The Fifth Discipline: The Art and Practice of the Learning Organization*. Random House: London.

Susskind, D. (2020). *A World Without Work: Technology, Automation, and How We Should Respond*. Allen Lane Penguin Random House Books: Milton Keynes.

Szostak, R. (2021). *Making Sense of the Future*. Taylor & Francis: London.

Taylor, A. (2024). *Higher Ground: How Business Can Do the Right Thing in a Turbulent World*. Harvard Business School Publishing Corporation: Padstow.

Varney, S. (2021). *Leadership in Complexity and Change*. De Gruyter: London.

Visnji, M. (2019). Apple vs Microsoft – Revenues and Profits 1995 to 2015 in *Revenue and Profits* https://revenueandprofit.net/apple-vs-microsoft-revenues-and-profits-1995-to-2015/

For Product Safety Concerns and Information please contact our EU
representative GPSR@taylorandfrancis.com
Taylor & Francis Verlag GmbH, Kaufingerstraße 24, 80331 München, Germany